Other books by Wayne Greenhaw:

The Golfer, a novel, 1968

The Making of a Hero: Lt. William Calley and the My Lai Massacre, 1971

Hard Travelin', a novel, 1972

Watch Out for George Wallace, 1976

Elephants in the Cottonfields: Ronald Reagan and the New Republican South, 1981

Flying High: Inside Big-Time Drug Smuggling, 1984

ALABAMA

ON MY MIND

Politics, People, History, and Ghost Stories

By Wayne Greenhaw

Published
By
Sycamore Press
3239 Lexington Road
Montgomery, Alabama 36106

ISBN 0-944404-00-6

Contents

For my stepfather, Andrew D. Brown,
and my father-in-law, Julian Maddox,
two who love their Alabama.

Beginning

In 1936, a visiting professor from upper-state New York taught English at the University of Alabama. During his year-long stay here, Carl Carmer traveled from the Tennessee River Valley to the bayous of Mobile County. When he went back north he wrote a book about his travels entitled *Stars Fell On Alabama*.

When I first read *Stars* as a teenager I was enchanted by the writer's views of our state. Later, while visiting my friends Borden and Babs Deal at their home in Sarasota, Florida, I met Carl Carmer. He was then more than eighty years old, but he remembered Alabama fondly. He asked about several people and talked about his teaching tour in Tuscaloosa.

Much later, after Carl Carmer died at his lovely home near the Hudson River, I wrote about the fiftieth anniversary of the book's publication. Only a few people remembered that it had been a book; they remembered only the song.

It had been Carl Carmer's words that had provided inspiration for the song, and it was his images: "Alabama felt a magic descending, spreading, long ago. Since then it has been a land with a spell on it — not a good spell, always. Moons, red with the dust of barren hills, thin pine trunks barring horizons, festering swamps, restless, yellow rivers, are all part of a feeling — a strange certainty that above and around them hovers enchantment — an emanation of malevolence that threatens to destroy men through dark ways of its own," that echoed through my own mind when I came down to the nitty-gritty work of putting together the enclosed pieces.

I hope to tell something here that is personal yet strangely universal. It is definitely Alabama, because I am Alabama. I was born in what Carl Carmer called The Red Hills. I was raised in

3

what he termed The Foothills in Shelby County and later Tuscaloosa. And I have lived most of my adult life in what he called the Conjure Country of Montgomery.

Born near Town Creek on the Tennessee River, my parents and grandparents were a part of the beginning of this state. My mother's father was a first generation Irish-American, born in South Carolina, and rode a bicycle next to a slow-moving wagon across the countryside to the piney woods of south Alabama near Florala. Mother's mother's people came to the North River country above Tuscaloosa after their travel-hardened forefathers fought to make their way through the wilderness, finally settling on that sandy soil. My father's people had first settled in Williamsburg, where John Greenhow was a tea merchant and a bottlemaker. When an offspring moved to the wilderness of the western mountains of North Carolina the name was changed by the slip of a country clerk's pen and it was carried on to Tennessee and later to north Alabama. On the way to the southwest of that day, my grandmother's great-grandfather, Robert Montgomery, was killed by a British musket at the battle of King's Mountain. After the Revolutionary War his children inched on southward, my grandmother's grandfather, who lived through the entire Nineteenth Century, brought his family to the banks of the Tennessee River where some of the family still live today.

Carl Carmer wrote about talking to old black people in villages along the Tombigbee River. These people told him about a story passed down from their fathers' fathers, when long ago a shower of stars fell on Alabama, changing the land's destiny. "What had been written in eternal symbols was thus erased — and the region has existed ever since, unreal and fated, bound by a horoscope such as controls no other country," Carmer wrote. He wrote of Alabama "as a strange country in which I once lived and from which I have now returned."

I write about it as a part of it, accepting now and forever the strangeness, the beauty, the reality and the delight as mine. One who has walked through the shadows of the deep, deep gulleys of Little River Canyon beneath the high rocky bluff of Buck's Pocket or across the ridges atop the wooded splendor of Cheaha where there are places three-hundred-feet high covered with water-smoothed pebbles has indeed felt that something strange once happened here. A barefooted prospector in the crystal cold December

4

Creek in Coosa County was panning for gold in 1967 when he told me about "something deathly evil once twisted and turned this land the likes of which it has never seen before or since." He believed it had been a battle between God and the devil that had turned the land inside out.

I will simply echo Carl Carmer's old black people, who perhaps got the shower of stars after the hand-to-hand combat.

What Is Alabama?

It's our place and a state of mind.

It's a rock-laden hillside in St. Clair County under which huge caverns hold the ghosts of yesteryear's gangsters. It's remembering what an old man told me about dice tables being set up in cathedral-like rooms beneath the earth's surface. He said that back in the '20s and '30s, people from Atlanta and Nashville and Birmingham would come down all dressed in their finery and converge on this literal underworld scene and a band would play swing music in the perfect acoustics and hundred-foot-high purple velvet drapes hung next to the natural rock formations.

It's listening to another old man tell about wild times while running for public office over the highways and byways of the state. He said nobody ever stood as tall or stooped so low to help all the people as that giant from Coffee County. He was Big Jim, the little man's friend.

It's a long white beach that stretches east to west and overlooks the clearest blue-green Gulf water. It's humming along with the strum of a stranger's guitar while a fire burns brightly and warmly on a brisk January night in the Flora-Bama bar while millions of stars flicker clearly overhead.

It's being a kid in the woods above Birmingham in the cabins of Camp Winnataska with older counselors telling stories of murder and mayhem. It's being unable to sleep and listening to the sounds of the woods that later haunt your dreams.

It's being eight years old and walking behind a mule and plow and old man and feeling the rich black dirt ooze between bare toes. It's getting hot and sweaty, "helping out," and tasting the metallic sweetness of ice water from a quart jar or galvanized dipper.

It's smelling the dank dustiness of a basement poolhall with all of its yesterdays mixed together in the aroma of stale cigarette butts, old tobacco smoke, unemptied beer cans, fresh chalk squares and talcum. It's listening to bragging talk around a green felt rectangle, and the tapping toes of a shark swaggering from corner to corner to see every possible angle on an eight-ball shot.

It's listening to rousing speeches on the square in Scottsboro on First Monday. It's remembering the towering figure of "Big Jim" leaning forward under the shade of an oak and telling 'em how this state needs a man who "ain't bought and sold by Big Mules from Birmingham."

It's sitting on a hard bench under the naked rafters of Old Nazareth Church in north Tuscaloosa County and watching a preacher ring the very essence of poetry from a Biblical verse he snatches from the humid summertime air. It's watching that very same preacher sing a song of praise for Paul and Luke and John while sweat pours from his brow and drips onto his coatless chest.

It's being so tired your eyelids weigh a ton as you fight to stay awake at three o'clock in the morning in the Senate chambers of the State Capitol while some lawmaker filibusters through the night. It's the resonant sounds of the voice of Senator Pierre Pelham of Mobile, pointing his finger toward Birmingham and declaring, "Before dawn the seven pillars of wisdom that have ruled this state will crumble!" And his voice echoed in those hallowed walls.

It's standing in Legion Field and watching red-and-white and orange-and-blue players gallop out and prepare for ceremonial combat not unlike tournaments in days of chivalry. It's arriving at the Stafford Hotel while it's still dark but knowing you're fifteen or twenty minutes late and seeing that man with the strong nose and powerful jowls leaning over a smoking cup of coffee and a yellow pad. It's trembling inside at his first grumbling word, because you know you'd do anything just to please The Bear, because he's the greatest. You wait and watch the yellow pad where he's playing a game with X's and O's.

It's holding a lady's hand while Jimmy Buffet sings like no one else has ever sung, *Stars Fell on Alabama,* and you know that melody will last forever.

It's walking down a sidestreet where Zelda and Scott once trod, sitting on a fender at midnight and tipping a toast to Hank, alone on an Oakwood hillside, or feeling a loneliness at the simple grave in the huge cemetery in Birmingham where The Bear lies forever.

It's being reminded of greatness at the simple little cottage in Florence where Helen Keller experienced the touch of water, or standing before a pew and looking up at that oak pulpit where Dr. Martin Luther King Jr. preached in the little brick church on Dexter Avenue, or feeling the beauty of a cool spring breeze while sitting on the azalea-touched steps of Oakleigh, or talking with a peanut farmer on the porch of a country store in the Wiregrass.

It's politics and perfume, hills and hollows, coon dogs and greyhounds, plowing mules and thoroughbreds, fox-hunting in central Alabama and hot-ballooning over the Tennessee River Valley.

Alabama is all of us, a collective group of individuals who love our place as well as our state of mind.

Alabama Politics

Politics, they say, makes strange bedfellows.

After having covered Alabama politics for thirty-some-odd years for various newspapers, magazines, radio and television stations, a journalist knows the people like they are family. There are the ones of which you are proud and others who are the black sheep, and you don't turn your back on any of them.

* * *

The first politician I knew was James Elisha "Big Jim" Folsom, a giant of a man who stood six-feet-six-inches and wore size fifteen-and-one-half shoes and whose hat would swallow my head even now.

The first time I saw him was in downtown Northport where I was riding in the cab of a pickup with my Granddaddy, a medium-sized man with thick shoulders and a heavy head and who walked with a limp because of an earlier injury and because his hip had shrunk with rheumatism, and with my Great Uncle Baxter Norris, a north Tuscaloosa County farmer and grand countryman who was more than six-feet tall himself and skinny as a rail.

Folsom lumbered down the sidewalk in an ill-fitting suit. The coat hung down nearly to his knees. Seeing us, he burst into a grin. "Uncle Bub!" he exclaimed, reaching out toward Granddaddy.

"Governor," Granddaddy greeted.

I saw the sign of a scowl cross Uncle Baxter's face and then disappear. Baxter Norris, my grandmother's brother, was one of those men who lived off fresh pork, garden vegetables, cornbread, piles of eggs and grits and bacon for breakfast, and never showed

11

one ounce of fat. He could walk at full gait all night when the hounds were chasing a coon through the hills and hollows.

After he shook Baxter's hand, Folsom lifted me up. "How you doing, young man?" he said. And he waited.

That was the first time I can remember an adult asking that question and seemingly wanting an answer. Most just asked it and went on about whatever else they were a-mind to say.

"I'm doing good, sir, if you'll let me down," I said. I felt rather silly, his holding me up like that.

He laughed heartily and lowered me. "I like a boy who'll speak his mind," he said.

Then he invited us to a barbecue on the next day. "It'll be up at Dee's place on the river," he said. "I want y'all to come." He looked down and into my eyes. "And I want you to come too, son."

I glanced up at Granddaddy, who nodded slightly.

"In the meantime, I believe I'll do a little cavorting with the boys," Folsom said, and he stepped widely across the street toward the drug store.

Granddaddy and Uncle Baxter went on about their business, and that afternoon we headed back into the country where they lived.

I asked Granddaddy if we could go to the barbecue.

"I ain't going," Baxter said shortly. He said he had little use for the likes of Jim Folsom or Dee Cunningham.

I had seen Cunningham before, and I wanted to see him again. He was among Tuscaloosa County's weirdest people, as far as I could see. He was a country landowner. He lived in the North River Valley (where the north end of Lake Tuscaloosa is now situated), and he owned several thousand acres of land, and he was known as one of the best behind-the-scenes political organizers in west Alabama. He was a big man. He was tall and heavyset with loose, fatty jowls. He had small blue — almost aqua — eyes set into a large face. He let his dark hair, which was by now graying, grow its full length. When it was not knotted into a bun on top of his head, it flowed down his back all the way to his waist. And, when he wasn't wearing loose overalls, he wore long flour-sack dresses. Once several years back, I had seen him coming out of the Tuscaloosa County Courthouse with the hair combed out and the flower-print dress hanging down below his knees to just above the brogans on his big feet. Needless to say, he was about the strangest sight I'd ever seen on these streets.

On Saturday, Nanny got fixed up, I put on my good checked shirt and my Sunday shoes, and Granddaddy buttoned his shirt up to the neck. It seemed that Granddaddy drove forever past the Samantha School, where he had conducted political rallies with *Tuscaloosa News* columnist Bob Kyle and local politicians like State Representative A.K. "Temo" Callahan.

The big frame house skirted by a wide porch sat up on an oak-shaded rise. Cars were parked all under the big trees where not one sprig of grass was allowed to grow. Out of the darkness behind a screened door popped the owner himself, Dee Cunningham, and I know when I saw the long hair and the dress and the heavy shoes I tried to hide inside the car.

Cunningham greeted us. Nanny, a broad, healthy woman with a totally open country face, smiled deeply and said, "Dee, if you're not a sight!" And Cunningham smiled the same way and clasped Granddaddy's hand and led us to the crowd in the back, where people were standing and talking and drinking, where a hog was being cooked on coals in a pit that flourished with a delicious and tantalizing odor, and where "Big Jim" stood taller than everyone else.

I hung around on the side while Granddaddy and Nanny mixed. I heard Granddaddy ask "Big Jim" about problems country people had had with getting electricity, and the former governor said he'd make sure that problem was solved when he went back in. "The biggest problem is these folks we got in power right now," Folsom said. The governor was Gordon Persons from Montgomery. "They don't care one whit about y'all out here in the country. They don't care enough to even come out here and ask. And I'll tell you something else . . ." And he was off and talking.

Granddaddy said it was the absolute truth that Folsom had provided farm-to-market roads when he was governor in the 1940s — just like he promised he would.

Leaning against the side of a Studebaker, Folsom, lifting a pint fruit jar filled with something that didn't smell like iced tea, said, "Ol' Big Jim never promised y'all a thing he didn't deliver on. You'll tell 'em that, won't you, Uncle Bub?" Everybody who knew him called Granddaddy Uncle Bub.

13

Folsom went through a long list of intricate legal situations he had supervised while governor. I didn't understand half of what he was saying and didn't really listen. But I did keep my eyes on the big, handsome man. He had a head full of fine dark brown hair. He had eyes like burning embers. And he had a mouth that wouldn't wait for talking. Every ten or fifteen minutes a girl came out of the house with a new pint jar filled to the rim with ice and whatever it was he was drinking. After about the third or fourth one I saw him drink down, he started talking about how the opposition had tried to get him.

"You know they talk about ol' Big Jim up north as Kissin' Jim," and he laughed loudly and slapped his knee. "*Life* magazine had me kissin' some pretty little ol' girls up in New York. They had 'em all lined up there when we got out of the helicopter and said I could kiss 'em, and I kissed 'em. Now they're calling me Kissin' Jim," and he laughed again.

I saw Nanny moving away in the crowd. After several more pints full of the amber liquor, Folsom began slurring his words. "Why, we'd a-done a whole lot more than we did if them no-account do-nothing legislators would-a done anything. They don't do nothing but try and catch ol' Jim drinkin' and having him put in jail." Many years later I discovered that state troopers had arrested him for driving while intoxicated outside Birmingham and at his trial several friends testified they had seen him only a few minutes before his arrest and he was sober. It looked as though the trooper was trying to set him up because it was his word against a half-dozen Folsom friends. Folsom was found not guilty.

With still another pint jar he talked on and on about the "do-nothing legislators," saying it was that branch of the government that had tried to stop Andrew Jackson from doing what was right back in the 1840's.

After his speech became very slurred and his eyes glazed and he could not hold himself erect, it became evident that he saw someone he recognized. He blinked his eyes. Just then his voice became louder and clearer.

"Of course," he said, "all the legislators aren't bad. There are good ones. And the best is A.K. 'Temo' Callahan of Tuscaloosa."

At that very moment, the state representative stepped up. Folsom grabbed his hand. "The honorable 'Temo' Callahan," he said, and a moment later his host and several others assisted the former governor into the back seat of a nearby Cadillac.

For the rest of the evening, while we enjoyed the succulent barbecue, the big man snored. You could hear him all over the field. And every time I looked that way I saw two huge feet poked out the open rear window of the long car.

Later Granddaddy told me Jim Folsom was a prince of a fellow who occasionally drank too much. Granddaddy said he'd done more for the poor farmer than any other governor. In the spring Folsom whipped the whole field of candidates without a runoff.

Big Jim Campaigns

Springtime in Tuscaloosa lightens the city. There is a literal change in the atmosphere. The honeysuckle grows stronger. The musty stench of the Gulf States paper mill in Holt hangs in the air in the early morning and then disappears by afternoon. The buds on the great Druid oaks bloom like flowers.

In the early spring of 1962, while the sun was going down and the afternoon air was breezy and light, we sat on the screened porch of the framed two-story house on 11th Street. With me were the owners of the house, my good friends, Borden and Babs Deal, the novelists.

We had exchanged coffee mugs for beer cans, and the air was even lighter.

Borden and Babs were expansive people. Both were private people, artists who worked alone, communicating between their brains and the typewriter, and after work was finished they liked to talk about whatever interested them.

Borden was a large, thick man. He had the hefty shoulders of a man who'd walked many a mile behind a mule and a plow when he was growing up on a farm near Pontotoc in the north Mississippi hill country. He also had a stringy red goatee and a wisp of a mustache below heavy lips and the strong nose of his Choctaw ancestors.

Babs had been a Hodges from Scottsboro. About seven years younger than Borden, she had a high forehead and black hair and strong brown eyes. When she talked her words came out in a high-pitched nasal singsong, drawing word pictures of her subjects.

Borden had hit the road when he was only a teenager. Known as Sierra Red, he told his special friends about that lonesome time on the rails out West during the Great Depression. In late-night sessions on this very porch where we now sat, he told in detail about hanging to boxcars while blizzards beat against him, reaching the far side of the Rockies with fingers numb and frostbitten.

Borden went into the Navy and afterwards entered the University of Alabama because Dr. Hudson Strode taught creative writing there. He wrote a short story in that famed class. It was called "Antanaes," and it won *Story Magazine's* college short fiction award, and later was included in *Best American Short Stories.* During the 50s, 60s and 70s, that story was picked up by books published from California to Sweden and Australia to Austria.

Borden's first novel, *Walk Through The Valley,* was published by Scribners and Sons after it had been turned down by a dozen New York houses. It was praised in *Time* and went through several printings.

In the early 50s Borden was awarded a Guggenheim Fellowship to study and write about the beginnings and development of the Tennessee Valley Authority.

Living in his wife's old home place in Scottsboro, Borden began work on what became *Dunbar's Cove,* a novel which hit the bestseller lists, was published in more than a dozen foreign languages, was condensed for Readers' Digest Books, and was combined with north Alabama's William Bradford Huie's *Mud On The Stars* to make the film *Wild River.*

Babs gave birth to two children in Scottsboro, Ashley and Brett, and a third in Tuscaloosa, Shane, and also wrote her first novel, *Acres of Afternoon,* which became a success in both hardcover and paperback.

As we sat on the porch in 1962, Borden began outlining his latest product. This was to be a political novel which, he said with strong enthusiasm so that there would be absolutely no misunderstanding, "will *really* be about politics. It won't be like *All The King's Men* the way *that* novel is phoney and misrepresents Willie Stark as a governor. This will really get into the politician's mind and will show what a politician is all about. It will *really* be about politics."

The first thing he was going to do, he said, was call their old acquaintance, Miss Ruby, who was Ruby Folsom Austin Ellis, the sister of former Governor James Folsom, who had said he was going to run for an unprecedented third term as governor.

All of a sudden, Borden and Babs began to recollect that time several years ago when Miss Ruby showed up right here on this porch.

All of us were inside at the time. We were having drinks and talking.

There was a loud knocking at the front door.

Borden frowned. He looked around at each of us. Several other students were sitting on the couch next to me.

The knock came again — louder this time.

He cracked the door.

A large person pushed against the door, swinging it open. "Hey, honey," the loud voice announced. "I'm Ruby Folsom."

She was a big lady with shoulders almost as wide as Borden's. After her she pulled a small, pretty brunette with frightened doe's eyes.

"You remember me," she said. "This is my daughter, C'nellia." Ruby literally shimmied in her dress that fit snugly to her ample middle. "Where's your bathroom, honey?" she asked.

Borden no sooner glanced in the direction than she rushed past him, entered, and slammed the door behind her.

She left the awkward young woman standing in the open front door with a guitar case in her hand.

Babs moved to Cornellia Ellis, introduced herself, and then went around the room with names.

When Miss Ruby burst from the bathroom, she carried a mound of clothes. She shimmied again and let out a deep breath. "Wheee!" she exclaimed, stuffing the loose clothing into a large handbag. "I thought that girdle was going to cut me in two!" Then she glanced around, grinned from ear to ear, and said, "You got a drink?"

Babs fixed her a tall bourbon and water and Cornellia a Coke. Ruby sat next to me, slapped my knee, and said, "You're a right nice-looking young fellow."

With her drink, she sat back and said, "Mr. Deal, I brought my girl, C'nellia here, to let you hear her sing. She's got the talent to be on Broadway."

Within the past few weeks the word had been publicized from New York that Borden's novel, *Insolent Breed,* would be made into

19

a Broadway musical. There had been several stories to that effect in *The Tuscaloosa News* and *The Birmingham News*.

Ruby drained the first drink quickly. With a second filled to the rim, she commanded, "C'nellia, sing, honey!" And Cornellia began nervously taking the guitar from the case.

She sang several country numbers in a timid voice, chording the guitar in the background.

Borden, who always liked to perform, took out his own guitar and played along with her. They sang several together, both off-key, and one did not have to be a music critic to know they would not be appearing together in a successful musical.

Before they left several hours later, Borden promised he would mention Cornellia to the producer of the show which eventually did open on Broadway under the title *A Joyful Noise*, with John Rait as star. It lasted for little better than a month but later was produced more successfully in Las Vegas as a musical revue.

In early 1962, Borden talked again with Miss Ruby, who called her brother on his behalf. Borden had indeed talked to the producer about Cornellia, and he had sent her to see another producer in Nashville who put her in several traveling shows there. Miss Ruby had not forgotten.

Several weeks later, I went with Borden to Scottsboro to hear "Big Jim" make his first speech of that year's campaign at the First Monday trade day.

On the way up Borden talked and talked about what he was looking for: "I want to create a man who is the personification of politics. I want him to be an everyman in the political world. Not simply a liberal or a conservative, he must be able to change color at will — a chameleon — without being hypocritical about it. He must be able to take a stand but have the common sense to compromise without losing face."

He went on and on, and as we were going over the hills and through the valleys of Jackson County, nearing Scottsboro, I began to see as a young writer what Borden was doing: he was using me as a sounding board while he was creating this character, who became known in his creative subconsciousness as John Bookman.

That Sunday night at the Holiday Inn we sat up late sipping beer and talking with some of Borden and Babs' old friends there, including the author Bill Heath, who had written a marvelous suspense novel entitled *Violent Saturday,* from which a better-than-average motion picture of the same name starring Richard Widmark had been made. "I don't think you're going to find a politician in the crowd tomorrow who will fit your description," Heath said. Borden said, "Probably not."

On the next day we went to the town square. We followed one after the other. A young man from south Alabama named George C. Wallace was a feisty one. He was like an angry bulldog as he faced the crowd. He told them, "The federal courts are trying to take over our life down here in the South. They're trying to tell us who we can go to school with and who we can't. They're trying to do what the British did to our ancestors in England, and that's why they came to this country: for freedom." The people applauded. He had crowd appeal. No doubt about it. After the talk, he went into the crowd and reached for the hands like a hound dog on a strong scent.

"Big Jim" stood up there and leaned toward the crowd and carried the microphone with him. He was a great big humble giant. He had a baritone drawl that still sounded pure and knowledgeable. "I want to make this state great, just like we worked on it four years ago and twelve years ago. We had our time, and we did good for you. We made sure you had jobs, and we built roads for you. Why, when I went into office in 1947, there was less than five miles of paved roads in Jackson County. Look at it today. You've got more than one-hundred miles of farm-to-market roads here. And we're not finished . . ." The people clapped. They hollered, "You tell 'em, Big Jim. We're with you." He grinned like a possum eating strawberries. "They say ol' Big Jim didn't treat you right." And they shook their heads and shouted, "That ain't true, Big Jim! That ain't true!"

They had come down off Sand Mountain, out of the coves along the dammed-up Tennessee River, and from the little wide places in the roads that he had built for them. They knew this man better than they knew George Wallace or any of the others. He told them he was "the little man's big friend," and they applauded louder.

Following Folsom was State Senator Ryan deGraffenried from Tuscaloosa. He was a clean-cut young man with sandy hair and bright eyes. He said he was "offering good government, cooperation from the Tennessee River Valley to Mobile Bay, and the prospects for new and better and bigger industry all across our great state." His was a promise of progress. And again the people applauded.

21

From Scottsboro we followed the Folsom entourage to Huntsville for a late afternoon rally where he repeated his speech from that morning. And that night we ended in Decatur.

Sitting in a room on the second floor of the Holiday Inn, Folsom kicked off his shoes and leaned back and sipped a cold one. Letting the foam evaporate on his lips, he breathed deeply and said, "Lord, that's good after a hard day of campaigning."

After we'd had steaks and potatoes in the dining room, we drank another beer. Borden asked, "Reckon it's going to work this time, Jim?"

Folsom grinned just like he had in front of the crowd. "Hell, boy, I don't know," he said. "I never do know. Back there in 1946, I carried a suds bucket and a mop around to every courthouse in the state and declared they all needed a damn good cleaning. Well, they did, and the people knew they needed it. They saw ol' Big Jim standing up there. I was taller and better lookin' than any of the rest of 'em. And I told 'em the truth: that I was for them, that I'd work for 'em, and that no damn Big Mule from Birmingham would tell me what to do and what not to do. By Big Mule I meant the big shots from the Alabama Power Company or the three-piece-suit boys from Pittsburgh who ran U.S. Steel or the hotshots who closed down the mines in Walker County.

"Back then I had a man with me named Gould Beech who was about the best political-thinking man I've ever seen. And I had another named Aubrey Williams who ran the *Southern Farmer* magazine and who used to work up in Washington with President Franklin Delano Roosevelt and the Farm Security Administration and the Rural Electrification Administration. Those two boys knew more about campaigning and getting things said — and communicated — than any other two dozen workers I've ever seen in this business. Now ol' Aubrey's dead, God bless him. And they've got Gould Beech out in Texas callin' him a Communist of all things. That's about the worst thing I've ever heard. He's no more a Communist than I am. He's a great American. And a damn smart one, too."

Jim talked on and on. We listened. We took down every word, every thought, every idea. "When I talk about getting the Negro people to vote for me, by God, it's something I really believe in. I always have. I think we've got to have those folks in the mainstream of life. We've pushed 'em back in the corner too long.

We've got to let 'em have their rights as citizens of this country, just like you and me."

In his speeches that day and in the days to come, Folsom said, "It is an historical fact that the only way to maintain segregation is to keep it out of court. I have successfully pursued this course in the past (waiting and allowing Autherine Lucy, the first black to integrate the University of Alabama in the 1950s, to speak out against the Board of Trustees, and then expelling her as the chairman of that Board).

"There are certain basic liberties that we need to be concerned with in Alabama today. We need to watch out for restricting the liberties of women. Ol' Big Jim is the last man in Alabama who would want to restrict the privileges of women. Today in Alabama they aren't allowed to serve on juries, and for years I've been telling folks it is time for women to be extended this liberty.

"You won't find Big Jim using any minority group — women or otherwise — as a political football. It just isn't right, and I'm not going to now. Our white people and our colored people have lived together in harmony ever since we became a state. It has only been in recent years when outsiders — rabble-rousers — from outside the state as well as inside the state — have created discord."

This was taking on George Wallace face-to-face. While Wallace was declaring that if elected he would stand in the schoolhouse door to keep blacks out, Folsom said, "My record of preserving segregation has been the best of any governor. I stand today, as I have stood in the past, for complete segregation of races in schools.

"My own uncles from Alabama marched off, to the tune of 'Dixie,' to give their lives during the Civil War. Three of them were killed. One of my grandpas opposed the war and one favored it. That division remained in our family for many years."

Folsom talked on and on, using Civil War images and re-collections from that devisive history. He attempted in his own homespun manner to intellectualize the racist point of view expounded by his number-one opponent, Wallace.

During the next ten days, we followed the candidates from town to town. We stayed closer to Folsom than the others. It became obvious that Wallace's demagoguery, his promise to stand in the schoolhouse door and his finger-pointing toward Washington, was captivating the masses. When he lambasted the federal

23

courts for their heavyhanded encroachment into the private lives of citizens of Alabama, the audiences rang loudly with applause.

One night as Borden was sitting at the table in our motel room in some small north Alabama town, he said, "Folsom tries to talk sense, and that can get you in trouble in politics." Making notes about conversations and observations from a long day of riding with Folsom and listening to him, Borden was already seeing the final score on the tally sheet of his mind.

Within a few short weeks we were back in Tuscaloosa. The Folsom group went on to Montgomery for a night-before-election television show. That weekend, according to his campaign workers, Folsom relaxed in Mobile. He drank some bourbon, sat back, and waited. On the night of the last TV show, something happened to the taped thirty-minute show which was supposed to be aired. Folsom, the big and boisterous two-time governor, insisted that he go on live. On the air it was obvious to all of those watching that he had had too much to drink. He cackled like a chicken, chanted "Coo coo, me too!" saying that was what the other candidates were saying, and could not recall the names of all of his children as he introduced his family. On the next day many of the votes he had thought were his vanished.

Wallace ran first in the primary. DeGraffenried was a distant second. Folsom was a few thousand votes behind the young man from Tuscaloosa who went into the runoff with Wallace, who eventually took the Democratic nomination and had no Republican opposition in November. It was the beginning of the Wallace era.

During the following year, I paid many visits to Borden Deal's home. Between classes at the University of Alabama, I'd drop by. The typewriter would be clattering away. From time to time I read the words describing the season of politics that was created in the novelist's mind.

His political character became a man named John Bookman. He was a big man, like Jim Folsom. He had white hair and bushy eyebrows, a physical description unlike any we'd seen that spring with Folsom. The man was young and packed with ideas and ideals not unlike the young Ryan deGraffenried. Halfway through the book, which was called *The Loser* when it was published by Doubleday, John Bookman began making fiery speeches akin to those we had heard from George Wallace on the stump.

24

Deal went on to write two more political novels, *The Advocate* and *The Winner*, about John Bookman. Later the trilogy was published as *The New South Saga* in paperback.

Not long ago I went back and reread them and found once again that they provoked a special magic quality unlike any other political novels I have ever read.

It was interesting that after *The Loser* was published, reviewers in Miami and Tampa said that "Deal obviously knows Florida politics because he has the Gang down to perfection," reviewers in Georgia wrote that he knew Peach State politics because anybody with insider knowledge knew he was writing about Atlanta and the surrounding environs, and in Tennessee it was just as obvious that he was writing about Nashville and Memphis and what had gone on there with Boss Crump and his followers.

I felt that all were correct. Borden Deal had traveled with some Alabama politicians and from them found a realness that he was able to portray in his writing. He had that kind of wonderful talent.

He went on to write such bestsellers as *The Tobacco Men,* which he fleshed out from notes left by Theodore Dreiser. It told the story of the early days of the tobacco industry and how it grew through the struggles of individuals against great odds. *The Spangled Road* was a superior novel about life in a circus and how that world was disappearing. And his allegorical book of backwoods life in the Depression-torn South, *Dragon's Wine,* received accolades from domestic and European critics.

His panorama of music in the South from hill country bluegrass to rockabilly soul singing in *Insolent Breed* became another success and was made into the Broadway musical *A Joyful Noise* and finally became a Las Vegas revue of the same name.

He and Babs moved to Sarasota, Florida. In the mid-seventies they were divorced. Babs moved back to Alabama. But Borden remained in Sarasota until his death in January of 1985.

I went down and conducted a memorial ceremony on the banks of his beloved bay where his first Sarasota house, High Barbaree, sat at water's edge. With friends like David Warner of Tuscaloosa, and his children, Ashley, Brett, and Shane, he was remembered as a storyteller, a singer of songs, and a man of good will.

Meeting The
Fighting Little Judge

In the Prologue of my 1976 biography of Governor Wallace, published by Prentice-Hall, I wrote about how I met him.

To quote from that book, *Watch Out For George Wallace*, which was published during the heat of the campaign during the primaries:

I was fourteen years old when I met Circuit Judge George Corley Wallace in a small-town barbershop. At the time he was south Alabama campaign manager for former Governor James E. "Big Jim" Folsom, who was seeking a second term. My father, a traveling beauty- and barber-supply salesman, had always voted Republican in a country that adored Franklin Delano Roosevelt. But Daddy never minded telling anybody his political preference. That afternoon in the barbershop you would never have thought Daddy even knew how to spell Republican, much less vote it. It was hard to tell who talked more, but Wallace mostly talked about himself. He probably didn't say ten words about Jim Folsom. I do remember that he went on and on about how the people of Alabama were damned good and tired of the Yankees telling us what to do and when to do it. And I remember my father agreeing with every word.

After more than an hour in the shop, Daddy and I got back into his car, which always smelled of after-shave lotion and permanent-wave mixture. On our way toward the next town, Daddy said, "That man's not going to stop until he's governor of Alabama."

Almost two years later I met George Wallace for the second time. Again I was with my father, and we were in another barbershop in another small town in south Alabama. He was doing some business and taking me and my best friend to the Gulf Coast

27

for a week in the sunshine. When Wallace came through the door, he bounced straight over to me, his arm outstretched, and he said, "How are you, Wayne? Who's your friend?" And again, he and my father spent time bantering about what was on their minds.

I liked George Wallace. If I could have voted, I would have voted for him. I knew no other adult who remembered my name after meeting me only one time and not seeing me for two years. He was an impressive man.

When he stood in front of my father he looked like an erect dwarf. My father was tall and heavyset. Wallace was nearly a half foot shorter, his chin was thrust upward, his lips full but taut, and his hair slickly combed with a wave beginning at the top of his forehead and sweeping back.

Nearly ten years later, when I became a reporter for the Alabama *Journal* in Montgomery, I met Wallace the governor. He recalled the first two meetings and asked about my father, whom he called by name.

While I have attempted to report objectively about George Wallace during the years, in these pages I want only to give some personal impressions about him, the other politicians I have known, and the trying times through which they served.

In his campaigns in the 1960s, Wallace was known long before President Ronald Reagan as the Great Communicator. Whatever they might think about his stand in the schoolhouse door, his tirades against the federal government, and his "Segregation forever!" speeches, all of the journalists who covered him realized quickly that he could move a crowd to tears or tyranny.

Wallace loved to mock the big city newspapers of Alabama. He attacked *The* Birmingham *News* and *The* Montgomery *Advertiser* with as much fervor and jowl-twisting as he mocked *The Time* magazine and *The Newsweek* and *The* NBC network.

One Saturday morning during a campaign speech in a shopping mall parking lot in Opelika, Wallace had reached that portion of his speech when he was tearing into *The* news media. And this time, with his head cocked to the side and his words rolling out of his lips with ease, he said, "Why, there are representatives here from *The* New York Times, *The* Los Angeles Times, *The* Alabama *Journal*, and even some Red Communist representatives of *The Pravda*."

By this point in the speech, most of us had quit writing in our narrow spiral notebooks. We already knew all of the lines. Also, we didn't want this crowd which had been swept into a kind of frenzy with his fast-talking rhetoric to move in our direction. There were some pretty big fellows and some strong-jawed women in that crowd.

The only person who had not stopped writing was Wallace's own press aide, Jack House, who was standing to the side with his pen writing steadily.

The reporters eased back, away from Jack, leaving him in the open.

Wallace had already moved on to another subject when Jack looked up and saw the angry crowd of people looking directly at him.

He realized immediately that the crowd had obviously mistaken him for the reporter from *The Pravda* and sweat popped from his face.

Jack began moving toward the platform from which Wallace was continuing to speak.

From the platform, Wallace recognized that his man was in trouble. He raised his hands. "Now, ladies and gentlemen, I'm not talking about these reporters when I say they're doing us wrong. These reporters are good people. They've been with me several days, and they've been writing what I say."

By now Jack was helped onto the platform by two men wearing imitation straw hats with red, white and blue WALLACE around the band.

After that close call, Wallace cooled his speeches when he came to the press part. Jack House told him it was working "too well," and Wallace understood.

The Governor Arrives

Not long after Wallace came to Tuscaloosa and stood in the schoolhouse door he came back to speak to a local civic group at the Country Club where I was assistant manager.

I worked evenings at the TCC and went to school during the days. I worked with a wonderful manager, Charles Turner, who had operated recreational facilities for the U.S. Air Force around the world. And we had a super group of people who cooked, tended bar, made sure every guest was comfortable, and rarely complained.

The night before Governor Wallace arrived, I met with our staff. Most of these people were black. They lived in and around Tuscaloosa. They had experienced racist attitudes from white people most of their lives. Many had witnessed cross burnings from Ku Klux Klan Grand Dragon Robert M. Shelton's hooded bigots. Many had been frightened more than once by gun-carrying white groups. And many of these local workers expressed fear about what might take place at the Country Club when the Governor spoke to the local citizens. "He's not speaking to us," said one tall woman who had worked as a waitress and as an assistant to the chef. I told them I did not believe Governor Wallace would be rabble-rousing when he spoke, that he would be talking about his administration in Montgomery, and that he would be explaining details rather than raising emotions.

Apparently my words went only half-heard. An uneasy rumble stirred through the group. A tall man named Willie, who was a combination night watchman and janitor, shook his head. "I think we going to have trouble," he said.

"I don't think so," I assured them. "Just go about your business

31

as usual. Make sure everybody is served. Be friendly and cordial, as you always are."

They nodded their heads, but I did not see a show of great enthusiasm. After all, these people had lived through a springtime of seeing their town disrupted by a governor who put on a great show for national television, state troopers stopping them when they shopped downtown, and the KKK surrounding one of their churches on a Sunday night when they were holding a prayer meeting.

The large dining room of the turn-of-the-century clubhouse filled quickly that night. Several times during the twilight hours I walked around the rock, brick, and frame building. I stopped and smoked a nervous cigarette next to the swimming pool and looked out over the shadows of the golf course toward the Warrior River. For a moment I thought I heard the sounds of a tom-tom somewhere in the distance. I thought about Carl Carmer's *Stars Fell on Alabama*, which had been written about this place some thirty-five years earlier. He had stood where I stood. He had listened to a voodoo chant. He had visited a witch doctor's shack on the edge of the golf course. But I had looked many times before. The shack was now gone. Nobody knew anything about voodoo, and when I asked their eyes got big with wonderment. Now, I supposed, I was imagining the ghosts of the gothic past.

The four hundred guests were seated when the Governor arrived. His bodyguards came in first. They were a solemn-faced group. They were no-nonsense. They skirted the crowd. They checked out all entrances and exits.

Governor Wallace came in in a rush. He met me, again calling me by name, asked several questions about my father, and said his speech was only fifteen minutes long — then he had a meeting elsewhere.

Prior to taking the podium, Wallace asked if I would take him into the kitchen.

Open-faced, smiling, hand extended, he shook hands with every person inside the walls of the Country Club. He exchanged pleasantries with the woman who had been scared that he would not be speaking to her.

Moments after he spoke and left, Willie, the janitor and night watchman, stood on the front steps of the club. He looked after the lights that had already disappeared.

32

"What's wrong, Willie?" I asked.

"You reckon that was really him?" Willie asked.

"Wallace?" I said.

He nodded.

"Sure, that was Governor Wallace."

He shook his head. "I don't think so," he said.

"Why's that?" I asked.

"He was too nice," Willie said. "You know he shook my hand? He asked how I was doing. He asked if there was anything he could do for me down in Montgomery."

"That's him," I said.

"He didn't act like he didn't like me. He said he was *my* governor." His eyes continued to watch the dark and empty road.

"He is your governor," I assured him.

"I didn't vote for him," Willie said. "But he said he was my governor."

"It makes no difference whether you voted for him or not."

For a moment Willie said nothing. Then he said, "You know, I wish I had-a thought of something."

"What's that?"

"You know, something that he could do for me. If I could-a thought of just one thing, then I'd see whether he was my governor or not."

For a long time after that night, when the news came on in the bar,. Willie would linger at the doorway. He always liked to watch "my governor" whenever Wallace appeared at a press conference or a speech or whatever.

After I moved to Montgomery and came back to Tuscaloosa from time to time, my friends at the Country Club told me Willie did some powerful campaigning for Lurleen Wallace for Governor.

The Governor
Likes Gumbo

When First Lady Lurleen Burns Wallace tossed her bonnet into the political ring in 1966, she told several capital city reporters that she was nervous but confident.

Mrs. Wallace's first appearances showed anything but confidence. She was nervous. It was a plain and simple fact. She would speak for two or three minutes, tell everybody how glad she was they'd turned out, ask for their support, and turn the microphone over to her experienced husband.

As the spring primary continued, however, the First Lady from Northport, where Governor George Wallace had met her behind the counter of a five-and-ten-cent store, grew more and more confident.

Day after day, she spoke longer and longer. At a rally in Albertville, she told the folks how she planned to work actively to promote better facilities for the mentally ill after she was elected. At a speech before a crowd in Saraland, she said she wanted to promote the state's great waterway system. In Florence, she advocated more, better, and bigger state parks and said it was a shame that the Tennessee River was not available for the entertainment of more Alabamians.

She defeated the large field of Democratic hopefuls without a runoff. The Alabama *Journal,* the newspaper for which I worked, ran a headline above my article the day after her victory: "Lurleen Wins . . . By George." Then she faced Republican Jim Martin of Gadsden, who had won a seat in Congress in 1964 on the coattails of unsuccessful Republican candidate, U.S. Senator Barry Goldwater.

Shortly before her first outing as the Democratic nominee, I asked if I could accompany her and Governor Wallace to Bayou la Batre for the blessing of the shrimp fleet. I was okayed, and on Saturday before the Sunday when we were to leave, Mrs. Wallace called my wife and asked if she would join us. Back in those days private citizens could ride on the state plane or in state-owned vehicles.

The next day, Lurleen Wallace was a delight. She was animated, full of herself, happy to be the candidate, and talked most of the way south about how the campaign made her feel like "a whole person."

We landed at Mobile's airport, a trooper met us and chauffeured us into south Mobile County, and Governor Wallace became more and more excited as the traffic became thicker. "Look there, honey!" he'd sing out. "Look at that car! They've got your bumper sticker! There's another one! Look at 'em!" He grinned from ear to ear. "I tell you, honey," he said, and he half-turned in the front seat. "They love you!"

And they did. Thousands turned out. They shook his hand. But they shook her hand too. And they hugged her and told her how much they cared for her and how they had voted for her and would vote for her again.

In detail, Mrs. Wallace outlined how her administration would smash even the records set by her husband when it came to industrial expansion. And while he had provided elementary schools and institutions with $116 million in bond money, she would make sure that money would continue to be spent wisely.

After Mobile State Senator Pierre Pelham introduced him with a flamboyant flow of adjectives, Wallace smiled and said, "I guess this candidate's going to do things better than I did." Then he reiterated previous tales of The Profit Opportunity State and how it had flourished under his leadership.

Back in the car that afternoon, Wallace grabbed hands out the window. So did his wife. And when we were on the road the trooper radioed ahead for a car to go to Bailey's, the famous Mobile Bay restaurant, and put in three orders of West Indies salad, gumbo, and fried crab claws. Wallace said he wanted well-done humburger steak and french fries.

"Honey, you don't want gumbo, do you?" he said, showing a grimace.

"Honey, the Governor wants gumbo," Mrs. Wallace said. "She loves gumbo!"

And so we had seafood while Governor George Wallace ate his hamburger steak smothered in catsup.

While he ate hurriedly, Wallace said, "I wish *The Time* and *The Newsweek* could be with us now. They'd just love talking about my eating habits." And we all had a chuckle.

I covered most of Governor Lurleen's term in office. She kept her promises. The first thing she did was find time to visit Bryce Hospital for the mentally ill and Partlow School for the retarded in Tuscaloosa.

Although the administrators at Partlow wanted to spare her the agony of seeing the most debilitated student-patients, she insisted that she and the press wanted to see it all.

As we passed through the third or fourth dormitory-style brick building, the huge room smelling strongly of ammonia mixed with stale urine, a pudgy-faced overweight child bounded from a nearby playpen. Her hands reached out awkwardly. She had difficulty balancing her body on her feet. Her large eyes pleaded within her pale dough-like face.

Her fingers reached toward the Governor, who responded with open arms.

The girl moaned something, but nobody understood.

Governor Lurleen hugged the girl to her and patted her back.

As the girl was taken by two tender-touching orderlies, she said her words again.

We all heard her say, "Mama! Mama!"

The Governor squeezed her elbows to her body and tears melted from her eyes. She had to turn away and bite her lower lip.

Before the tears had been wiped away, she seized the moment. She spoke out loudly for reform of all mental health institutions in Alabama.

That night, when the people of Alabama saw her on television, nobody could argue with her. It was obvious that strong measures would have to be taken to right the wrongs in the state's mental health institutions.

However, she became sick with cancer and died before drastic measures were taken. During her husband's second term in the early 1970s, a class-action suit was filed in federal court. Wallace's old nemesis, U.S. District Judge Frank M. Johnson Jr., against whom he had campaigned in the 1960s, issued a far-reaching order that revolutionized mental health in Alabama and the United States, requiring minimum standards to be met by all public institutions. I could not help but think that she would have been pleased — even thrilled — by such a decision.

Not long after Governor Lurleen's inauguration in January of 1967, I arrived at the capitol early one morning. I planned to finish an article I had begun in the press room the day before.

As I entered on the south end of the main floor, I saw someone standing in front of the door at the far end of the hallway. As I got closer and closer, I saw that the silhouette was one with which I was familiar.

Instead of turning and going to the elevator in the rotunda in the center of the capitol, I stopped and tried to make out the figure. The woman was squatting, looking into the doorway to the Governor's Office, and I said, "Can I help you?" in a voice loud enough to be heard up and down the otherwise silent capitol hall.

"Wayne? Is that you?" The voice was that of the Governor.

"Yes, ma'am," I said. I walked in her direction. Governor Lurleen was standing alone in the hallway. She explained that she had awakened earlier than usual, decided she would come to work early, and found the door locked.

"But there are people inside," she said. She looked through the cracks in the venetian blinds inside the office. "It looks like they're having a party."

The women in the office were laughing and drinking coffee.

"I knock, but they won't come over here."

"They're probably afraid you're somebody else," I said.

She said she didn't have a key. She wondered how they got inside.

She followed me downstairs to the basement. That was in the days before there were offices in every corner of the basement. There was a back door there which led to a narrow stairway that came up in the small hallway outside the governor's inner office.

I showed her to the stair.

As I turned, she touched my arm. "I'd appreciate it if you wouldn't write about this," she said.

I nodded.

Until now, I have not written about it. But after the time and events that have passed, what harm would it do now? After that morning, she had her own key to the outside door. I never knew what she said to the people who worked for her, but I always felt that was the day she began being governor in more than name only.

The day of her funeral was a sad one for the state of Alabama. Everybody mourned. She was a lovely lady who worked hard for all people.

It was several years later, when I awakened very early one morning and went to Greenwood Cemetery at the end of Highland Avenue to visit the grave of a friend and have a moment to myself and my memory. I drove up the hill and around what was called Governor's Circle, where Governor Lurleen was buried, when I saw the black car.

Before I turned to go down a roadway where my friend lies, I saw him. Governor Wallace sat there. His face was long and sad. I am sure a tear streaked his face.

Our eyes met. I nodded. I went on. It was a silent time of remembering for him. There was no public here.

I never said anything about it. I never wrote about it. But in remembering him and her, I cannot help but think about that morning. It gave me a little something special to remember him, something soft and sad, something well worthwhile.

Montgomery: My Home Town

I fell in love with Montgomery.

When I moved to the oak and magnolia street of Gilmer in 1964, it was the grandest spot of my dreams.

I had spent most of my growing up days in Tuscaloosa, the Druid City, where everything was always at least slightly tinged with a smell of the paper mill and a polluted river. It was a wonderful city but not a dream city.

Montgomery was my first grown up home. With a friend, I rented a spacious old apartment furnished with hand-me-down antiques. It was in a massive mansion with four columns across the front on the corner of Gilmer and Frederick. I had my nook in the forties built-on bedroom and bathroom in the rear behind the large modernized kitchen. My roommate had a huge bedroom off the front hallway. And we could dropkick a football or chip a golf ball from our wall-to-wall carpeted living room into the dining room.

It was a wonderful house in which we had all of the downstairs. We played "Smile Awhile" on the stereo and thought about days when F. Scott and Zelda danced on these very floors. It was Fitzgerald who wrote that this place was "... a languid paradise of dreamy skies and firefly evenings and noisy street fairs — and especially of gracious soft-voiced girls who were brought up on memories instead of money."

At age twenty-four I heard those soft voices. There were young ladies from Huntingdon College. One especially caught my eye, and for the better part of a year we spent time together, going to the art shows, flea markets, walking the banks of the crooked river, and listening to the songs of the night.

There were others, and time flew by with the weekend parties and the flighty sounds of arguing people and the problems of a place in transition. We bedded down weary travelers who had walked from Selma to Montgomery. We filled the wall-to-wall carpeting with them and heard their stories from Harvard and Princeton and Yale and Georgetown. That night we met Sammy Davis Jr. and Harry Belafonte and Peter, Paul and Mary. In the crowded hall of an apartment in a house across Court Street from Sidney Lanier High School stood the red-haired troubadour Pete Seeger talking with Pulitzer Prize-winning historian C. Vann Woodward. People were talking about things that had happened and things that would happen, and the air was alive with the joy of worthwhile conversation. In the middle of a sea of young people and older people sitting on the floor was a slender man in a rocking chair. He rocked slowly and smoked an unfiltered cigarette between thin lips. His eyes were blue as Gulf water and his skin was loose around the jowls and heavy with a day-old stubble. He talked quietly about legal problems that existed in the Black Belt counties, problems that he would like to see faced by the multitudes like the great number of persons who would be marching in downtown Montgomery tomorrow for the Voting Rights Act. After a while, when he finished telling a story about a friend of his who was in jail in Russia for protesting against the dictatorship-style government there, I met him. This was his house. His name was Clifford Durr, and I believe he was the gentlest man I ever met.

He had served on the Federal Communications Commission under President Franklin Delano Roosevelt. When Roosevelt died at Warm Springs, Georgia, in 1945, it was said that he had a scrap of paper in his breast pocket on which he had written Clifford Durr's name and the U.S. Industrial Recovery Act. Insiders said Durr would have been appointed to direct wartime industry being put back into the private sector if Roosevelt had lived. Durr's friend, Harry Truman, became President after Roosevelt died. They talked frequently, and Durr had the greatest of respect for the President. On a Friday, Truman told Durr that he would never put into effect a loyalty oath, that he thought such was unconstitutional and against the dignity of man, but on Monday morning *The Washington Post* announced that such an oath had been ordered by Truman.

As soon as he could put his office into shape, leaving the absolute instructions on how to insure that at least one channel on television would be put aside as a public educational network, Durr resigned. Because of these efforts with the FCC, Alabama, his home state, had the first educational television network.

He and his wife, the former Virginia Foster, who had become a close friend of First Lady Eleanor Roosevelt and who had fought diligently through the years for such liberal causes as the abolition of the poll tax and women's suffrage and civil rights and voting rights for all citizens in the South, returned to Alabama. He practiced a little law and cultivated an inherited hillside in Elmore County which the family affectionately called The Pea Level.

He assisted several young black attorneys who were attempting to start a practice in Montgomery — Fred Gray and Charles Langford. When Rosa Parks was arrested for failing to give up her seat on a Montgomery city bus to a white man, Durr signed her bond. He worked with Gray and Langford and helped them to plan her defense with black leader E.D. Nixon. He said that "to make a difference," the case should be tried on its Constitutional merits, making sure all along the legal highway to the U.S. Supreme Court that certain evidence showing the unconstitutionality of the local segregationist law be proven.

During this time of discontent in Montgomery, Durr also defended a young white friend who had earlier been a student at nearby Huntingdon College. When Bob Zellner was arrested for trespassing on the campus of his alma mater, Durr challenged the local authorities. These authorities wanted to make an example of Zellner, whom they knew was a civil rights activist and an organizer of civil rights demonstrations. The law under which Zellner was arrested was later ruled unconstitutional, just as Durr had believed in the beginning. It set a precedent for other rulings during the 1960s and 1970s.

Once when I took a young lady with whom I worked to The Pea Level, Clifford Durr took us on a guided tour through the woods. In a pleasant sing-song voice, he told about the ghost of a Creek Indian who lived along the ridge where we walked. With hoe in hand, he cut a path for us to the rushing water of the creek that ran through the backside of his property. We sat on a big rock and he told other stories. On the way back, a snake zipped near his feet. He stood poised with the hoe cocked. "Shall I kill him?" he asked. "Oh, yes,

43

yes!" the girl said. Durr slammed down the sharp blade of his hoe. "Poor devil," he said. "Executed without due process." As it turned out, the snake was only a harmless black racer.

When I was covering Ku Klux Klan cross burnings in Prattville or Montgomery, Grand Dragons from Birmingham spoke out against "those Communist nigger-lovers, Clifford Durr and Aubrey Williams," and my chest swelled with the knowledge that I knew and admired these men. I knew neither could ever be communists.

Aubrey Williams edited the *Southern Farmer,* a magazine which promoted agricultural reform, the Resettlement Administration, and the Farm Security Administration. Williams was a fellow New Dealer. President Roosevelt had appointed him in the 1930s to direct the National Youth Administration. He was a man who believed the Constitution applied to all people, which branded him a liberal in those days.

I learned that Montgomery was a fickle lover. It had as many twists and turns to its personality as the black snake of a river that wound through its north side.

Montgomery had originally been two communities, East Alabama, which developed around a trading post in the northward bend of the Alabama River, and New Philadelphia, which grew up around another commercial establishment high on the bluff overlooking the great curve in the river. In that curve, almost halfway between the two original settlements, a landing wharf was built. Large paddleboats picked up cotton that had been picked, then moved southward through the Black Belt to pick up more raw material to deliver eventually to mill towns in the North where it would be spun into cloth. The underground tunnel through which the cotton was hauled became the northernmost boundary of Commerce Street, where some of the largest cotton exchanges in the world — Weil Brothers and Loeb & Company — were founded, flourished, and continued with success into the Twentieth Century.

When I came to know this area, it had fallen into disrepair. It was the stepchild of the growing town. Winos, derelicts, and curious young reporters stalked the dreary alleys. Union Street Cafe had the toughest coffee in town, brewed each morning in its antique urns, and the faces along the rustic counter mirrored tough times.

These people talked. I guess they wondered about the innocence and stupidity of youth. They told about times aboard the freight trains. One was a former professor from Auburn who had become disenchanted with the academic life — or it with him. He was an out-and-out alcoholic. His hands shook and his lips quivered. He drank the cheapest of wine — or canned heat — or bay rum; it made no matter, as long as it contained alcohol. Another was a laborer who kept saying he was between jobs, but when jobs came open in manufacturing plants in north Montgomery, he was never present to take a shift.

After my first year in Montgomery, when I worked with an experimental educational project at Draper Correctional Center in rural Elmore County, I got a job with *The Alabama Journal*. My first major story, covering more than a full page, told the tales of the riverbank people. It quoted them telling their story.

My managing editor at *The Journal*, Ray Jenkins, had just returned from a year at Harvard as a Nieman Fellow. He told fascinating stories about the greats of academia and journalism, and I knew it had been a wonderful experience for him, and it was one I aspired to. Ray was a tall, gentle man with long piano-player's fingers, a high brow that would go bald during the years, and the mind of a mathematician-poet. On one hand he was filled with nitty-gritty facts. He dissected the facts analytically, then he always managed to see the romance or terror beyond. He had been a member of a Pulitzer Prize-winning team of reporters and editors who had sought the truth after Attorney General-elect Albert Patterson was killed on the streets of Phenix City on the border between Alabama and Georgia. Phenix City had been known as the Sin City of the South with main streets lined with honky tonks, gambling dens and whorehouses. Patterson had won the state Democratic Party's nomination as Attorney General with the promise to clean up the filth and corruption, then he was gunned down, and marshal law was declared. Jenkins and his cohorts on *The Columbus Enquirer* across the Chattahoochee River in Georgia covered the facts of the death, the subsequent investigation, and the trial in Birmingham. His writings about the people involved, the complex political situation that led to the violence, and the behind-the-scenes world of crime became a textbook study of journalistic excellence.

Later Jenkins would leave Montgomery to become Special

Assistant to President Jimmy Carter in Washington, D.C., and then to occupy the chair once filled by H.L. Mencken at the Baltimore *Evening Sun.* His essays on life have been printed with consistency on the Op-Ed Page of *The New York Times,* reprinted in the *Reader's Digest,* and picked up by newspapers all across the U.S.

In those days, when I was learning my new home town, Ray Jenkins was my teacher. He gave superior advice, putting his finger directly on the problem and explaining it in the clearest of language. "Write exactly what you want to say," he said. "Don't write around something. Look at it, see it, then write it!"

He allowed me to go amongst the riverbank people and to come back to the offices on Washington Street and write about them.

Unlike so many other veteran newspaper people, Ray Jenkins never hid his excitement when we came into the newsroom with a really good news story. His eyes grew larger, almost like a child's, and he wanted to know more.

One Monday morning in the mid-1960s, I came into the office very early. I had been out almost all night. I had received a telephone call early on Sunday morning. It had been from a man who would not identify himself at first. "There's been a killing up here," he said. "Where's 'up here'?" I asked. "Elmore County. I know you cover some of the county stuff for *The Journal.* This was a killing that took place a few hours ago on the side of Highway 231. A white deputy sheriff hit a black man over the head. I saw it. Blood spurted everywhere. They took him to the Elmore County jail, but he was already dead when they got him there."

I repeated all of this to Ray, while he leaned back and put his long legs up and clasped his hands behind his head. When I finished, he asked three or four pertinent questions which I could not answer, but I made notes. I told him who I had seen and what I had found out beyond the first telephone conversation. Indeed, a black man who was on leave from the U.S. Army had died early Sunday. Authorities in the sheriff's office said James Earl Motley had died after he sustained lacerations to the head in a fall from the second-deck of a bunk in the jail. I read from my notes where I had interviewed family members and others who had been riding in the car which had been stopped shortly after 1 a.m. Sunday morning. Several had told me that Motley had been hit over the head with a

46

billystick by the deputy, that he had fallen to his knees, and then had been shoved into the deputy's car.

Jenkins nodded his head slowly. He said it sounded like a good story, but I needed to proceed with caution. "We're talking about the possibility of a man killing somebody," Jenkins said. "Don't let anything go uncovered."

A young black reporter for Montgomery radio station WRMA, Norman Lumpkin, who had come to Montgomery from Atlanta after he had learned broadcast journalism from a correspondence course, was also on top of the story. He was the first to report it that Monday morning. That afternoon he and I compared notes. There were some places he could go and I could not, some where he needed me for entry; we decided to share whatever we found.

Working with him, I discovered that Norman Lumpkin was already a savvy journalist. He asked every question and then some. He did not mind appearing silly or even stupid; he wanted the facts, and he probed deeply for them.

I learned also that when bullyboy whites in positions of authority attempted to push him around, Lumpkin would appear backwards and untrained. He would stumble over words I had heard him pronounce easily and smoothly only moments earlier. One evening that week when we were driving to a black district outside Wetumpka, I asked him about his appearance when a deputy questioned him harshly. He grinned. "They like to think we're stupid," he said. "If they think it, they know I don't know anything they don't know. Then they talk a lot more. And my tape recorder is always on."

A coroner's inquest was held later that week at a veterinarian's office. I was subpoenaed but could not sit and listen to other witnesses. The doors were closed to the press. An attorney for *The Journal*, M.R. "Rod" Nachman Jr., gave me an Alabama law to read stating that a reporter is not required to divulge his source. It was called the Hugh Sparrow law, because it had been tested back in the 1930s by the famous Birmingham *News* political reporter. Nachman also said that if the Elmore County authorities put me in jail for contempt, to call him for bail and he would be there as soon as possible.

My stomach was in somewhat of a knot as I walked into the room with the old sheriff, Lester Holley, a stone-faced veteran law enforcement officer with steely eyes and a gravel voice; the deputy sheriff who was being accused of hitting James Earl Motley, and the coroner, who was also the veterinarian in whose office they were sitting.

Holley, who had been sheriff for some thirty years, was a legend in his own time. He walked tall and was mean as his eyes warned. Blacks from every hill and hollow of the county were frightened of him. It was said that he didn't need to subpoena a black to court, he just put out the word that so-and-so would be expected at the county courthouse at 9 a.m. on Monday and the person would arrive at five-until-nine. That was standard operating procedure. It was also said that he had pistol-whipped more than one prisoner who would not talk.

He told me, "Have a seat, boy, and answer some questions for me."

I said that I could not tell them the names of the persons who had told me about the deputy sheriff who had arrested Motley, beaten him on the head, and carried him into the jail.

Holley looked around at all four walls. "Now, boy, there ain't nobody else in here but us four folks, so it don't matter none what you tell us. You tell, and we won't tell anybody you told . . . You know what I mean?"

With my hands shaking, I read the law to them.

"Aw, now, boy, we don't need all that. You just nod if I mention the name of the fellow who told you."

He called out several names.

"I know you want to cooperate with us. You look like a good citizen. All we want is to get at the bottom of all this foolishness. There's a bunch of niggers lying to beat the band, and my deputy here is getting hurt by all this stuff. I've been sheriff a long time and I'm not going to run again. I just don't need all this stuff."

But I said nothing.

They didn't arrest me.

Outside I was interviewed by Norman Lumpkin. Because I had been questioned, suddenly I was a part of the story as well as a reporter.

Back at *The Journal*, I wrote a first-person story telling about the questioning.

I also wrote a story from my interviews with Motley family members and the young women who had been with Motley on the night he died. They told about intimidating questions being asked by the sheriff and by the duputy. They held to their story.

By Thursday I had been up all night two nights in a row. I had interviewed a number of people. That morning, when I was awakened by Ray Jenkins from my sleep on the old couch in the newsroom, I had a story which began: "Three white men have told *The Journal* that they saw a white Elmore County deputy sheriff beat a black man over the head with a club, that the black man began bleeding, and that they saw the deputy carry the man's body into the Elmore County jail less than an hour later. 'He looked like he was dead,' one witness told *The Journal.*"

It was important that the witnesses, although unnamed, were white. Prior to this time, all witnesses quoted had been black. In this time of racial tension with demonstrations almost daily in downtown Montgomery, it had appeared to be a black versus white issue. Now, suddenly, there were white witnesses also.

By the end of the day readers across Montgomery were quoting the article and nodding their heads.

According to Elmore County District Attorney Upshaw G. Jones, the case would be presented to the Grand Jury there.

Nearly a week later, the Grand Jury brought a no bill in the case. That same afternoon, a federal grand jury in Montgomery brought charges against the deputy of violating James Earl Motley's civil rights under color of the law, or while he was acting as a law enforcement officer.

Several months later the deputy went on trial. During the trial one witness after another testified against the defendant. A state trooper who had answered his radio call that night told about the deputy's hitting Motley. "When he hit the man, what did you do?" asked the lawyer. The trooper's eyes watered. His voice shook. "What did you do?" the lawyer asked.

"I turned away," he answered.

The deputy sheriff took the stand in his own behalf and testified almost word for word to what the three white witnesses had told me earlier.

He was at a filling station on the Elmore-Montgomery county line when he saw this "car full of niggers going too fast up the highway."

When he pulled them over, on the first toehill of the Appalachians, he called for help.

James Earl Motley was in the back seat with a black woman. All four people in the car, the deputy said, had been drinking. When he told the driver to step outside, Motley "wised off." He got out of the car, walked toward the deputy, who pulled out his billyclub, a six-inch piece of leather into which a bar of lead had been stitched.

When Motley talked back to him, he said, "I told him, 'Nigger, keep your mouth shut!' and when he reached out to grab a hold of me, I hit him across the head."

He said Motley fell to his knees, reached up for him again, and he hit him again. Motley began bleeding.

The deputy put him into the car, where he bled more. He said he took Motley to the jail where he got help to lift him and take him inside.

During the night, he said, Motley rolled off the bunk and hit the top of his head against the concrete floor, where he lay until he died.

Asked if he sought any medical aid for Motley, the deputy said he didn't think Motley was hurt that badly. The deputy said he discovered Motley dead on the floor the following morning.

The jury found him innocent of violating Motley's civil rights.

That evening I told friends, including New York *Times* reporter Gene Roberts and Los Angeles *Times* reporter Jack Nelson and Jenkins, that I felt I had done all the work for naught. Roberts said, "No, you made the price of killing a black man mighty high in Alabama. I bet it'll be a while before another deputy sheriff does what that one did. He got off, but it cost him a lot of money."

From that series of stories I also came away with a very good friend. Norman Lumpkin went up north for a few years to work for a big-city radio station. When he came back he called from the Greyhound bus station. I met him and had a cup of coffee. "Guess what I'm going to be doing?" he said. I shrugged and sipped. "I'm going to be WSFA's token," he said.

He became WSFA's first black reporter. But he was nobody's token. Norman Lumpkin made a name for himself as one of the finest journalists in Alabama. He never gave up working diligently for the facts and the ultimate truth.

During these years I also became friends with a man who had been city editor of *The Montgomery Advertiser* during the bus boycott days of the early and mid 1950s. By now Joe Azbell was a regular columnist for *The Montgomery Independent,* and he knew more people in the capital city than anyone. When I was stuck on a name and a connection, I called Joe. He always had time for me.

Joe Azbell was a big man in many ways. He was tall. He had a big head and a great smile. When I wrote in my 1976 biography of George Wallace that Joe spoke with an endearing lisp, he informed me quickly that he was tongue-tied and that this problem had existed ever since he was a small boy and had been beaten by a grown up in his small town Texas home.

Life was worse than tough in that dust-whipped town during the Great Depression, and Joe left home when he was only eleven. He worked for a man on a weekly newspaper near Fort Worth, learning to set type. At night he educated himself by reading the classics given to him by the editor.

A few years later this young man with a superb photographic memory and a sharp wit and an ear for the English language found himself in the U.S. Army, stationed near Selma, Alabama. He was a person who learned quickly. It had been forced upon him early, and he saw it as a necessity for survival. He sought out the leaders of the town, sat down with them and listened to them, and he let them believe they were teaching him. Within a short period of time he knew the intricate ins and outs of Selma politics, who belonged to what factions, and who were necessarily fighting whom. He saw that it was not too unlike the small town politics he had known in Texas, just different people playing different positions; it was a game with which he quickly became more than proficient; it would, indeed, become part of his life's success.

Not only was he smart, Joe Azbell worked very hard at whatever he did. He not only put out a newspaper at Craig Field, in the evenings he wrote and edited a weekly newspaper in Selma. He also met and married a lovely young woman, Betty Johnson, who was a member of a prominent local family. Her actual father had died before she was born and later her mother married Johnson, who loved his stepdaughter and gave her his name.

After Richard F. Hudson, the publisher of *The Montgomery Advertiser,* became acquainted with Azbell's work, he offered the young man the job as city editor of the capital city newspaper. Azbell had a budding young family, was energetic and lively as a businessman as well as a newsman. He knew a story when he whiffed it, and once he tracked down the real killers after a young black man had been arrested for the rape and murder of a town white woman. It was one of those stories some southern editors simply dismissed and forgot. Azbell believed the young defendant's pleadings that he was innocent, followed through with hour upon hour of legwork, and proved himself a worthy investigator. After he found the real killer and turned the evidence over to local police, Azbell was not only awarded state prizes, his behind-the-scenes work became the subject of a nationwide television broadcast entitled *Pall Mall's Big Story* and he was personally introduced to the national audience.

In the early mornings before he went to work and late in the evenings, Azbell, then a tall and skinny young man, sifted through huge public dumpsters for pasteboard people threw away. The old adage, one man's trash is another man's treasure, became a truism for Azbell, who sold what he found to local manufacturers. This extra money not only helped take care of his growing family but was saved to be invested in local real estate.

His aging boss, Mr. Hudson, showed Azbell how he could develop his wealth. The young journalist also listened to an elderly real estate entrepreneur, Les Weinstein, and others. Before long, Azbell was using the knowledge he learned as editor to take possession of rental houses in poor sections of Montgomery simply by paying back taxes owed by absentee landlords. However, unlike many such landowners who actually moved through flooded north Montgomery in flat-bottomed boats to collect rent, Azbell helped his tenants and was seen on several occasions carrying them food and clothing.

In 1954, when the black community was about to call a black boycott, his old friend, black leader E.D. Nixon, called Azbell. They met at a clandestine spot, Nixon outlined what was about to happen, and on the following morning Azbell's story was headlined on page one. "I knew it would take the preachers and the newspaper to get the word out," said Nixon afterwards. "I knew some people didn't go to church."

During the years, like any good news person, Azbell developed a great spectrum of acquaintances. He also developed a number of verbal skills. After he left *The Advertiser* he became the most sought after local political consultant with the vast ability and certain knowledge of the ins-and-outs of central Alabama personalities. He also went back to his native Texas and became a political mover there, working during frequent plane trips to that country, where he met and impressed several religious leaders in Fort Worth, Dallas, and Tulsa.

From his faraway outpost in Montgomery, Joe Azbell produced tabloid-style newspapers which told the story of these religious leaders helping starving people, people fallen by natural and military disasters, and other work for humanity. He also wrote letters appealing to strangers out there in the heartland of America for monetary assistance in this work.

In the 1960s and early 1970s, Azbell also worked as a media consultant to the George Wallace for President movement. In 1968 he created the best political slogan of the times: Send Them A Message, and it became the battle cry of Wallace's Third Party forces.

Through the late 1970s Azbell continued his work for religious organizations, political candidates in Alabama, Texas, and Oklahoma, and advised Governor Fob James as a media consultant.

On the second floor of *The Advertiser* building I sat at the desk behind the large support post that came up from the basement through the first floor. Next to it was the water fountain at which everybody in the building seemed to pause at least once every day. Through a hole next to the support post came the fumes of the old lead-melting linotype machine downstairs that also made an incredible amount of clickety-clacking noise whenever it was being operated to set the type for the day's paper. It was quite a bit different — even another world away — from the wall-to-wall carpeting and the quiet air-conditioned atmosphere that prevails in the newsroom today. Back then the reporters typed like mad to the rhythm of the clanking sounds of the machines downstairs and the teletype machines of the Associated Press and United Press International that brought us the daily happenings from around the world. There was nothing quite like the excitement of a fast-breaking story from some faraway location as it fed into the big open room through these machines. When U.S. Senator Robert Kennedy was shot we got a slug that read: "U.S. Sen. Robert F. Kennedy (D.-N.Y.), a candidate for the Democratic nomination for president, was believed to be shot tonight after making a speech accepting victory in the California primary." It was datelined Los Angeles. Every minute or two more and more information was fed

53

over the wire, each time adding to that lead, until finally the lead was changed to state that Kennedy had been assassinated. It was a drama that unfolded every time a major event occurred.

Such was the drama of an election night in those days. It was even more exciting, because it was shared by many people — politicians and private citizens alike — who gathered in the newsroom to watch for the latest returns from across the state.

While I was not there in 1958, the original dapper dandy — the editor-in-chief of *The Advertiser* and *The Journal,* Grover Cleveland Hall Jr., told me about sitting with a nervous George Wallace in Hall's corner office just off the newsroom in 1958 when the returns of the first primary were coming in. Hall's secretary ripped off sheets of the AP or UPI copy from the machine, brought them into the office, and handed them to the editor. "I would then read them to Wallace, who was pacing the floor like a virtual prisoner awaiting the executioner. I enjoyed tantalizing him with the bits and pieces of returns as they came in," Hall recalled.

As Hall told it in his tell-a-story rhythm, his voice rising and falling with the dramatic elements of the tale, I could easily see the two of them in the office: Hall leaning back in his chair behind the big neat desk next to the wall of bookshelves, Wallace pacing back and forth and wringing his hands together and trying to guess what county's election results could be coming in next.

Hall, who had twinkling eyes and a handsome F. Scott Fitzgerald face, remembered Wallace becoming more and more despondent that night as State Attorney General John Patterson took the lead and held it. Early on, Bay Minette publisher Jimmy Faulkner held second place. But in the final analysis, Wallace's rural vote came in and he was in the runoff.

While all of this was happening, Wallace asked Hall how he could use his strengths and come out of the gate at a full gallop. He knew now that he had finances. In Alabama, if the politician is in the Democratic runoff, the money people are following him around to fill the coffers. Until the early morning hours, Wallace and Hall worked on themes of several speeches for the runoff.

During the next week Wallace promised to build more trade schools, develop a system of junior colleges, and build more and better highways.

In the meantime, Patterson said nothing. For the first time, television was used effectively in a political campaign. His people ran spots using film clips from *The Phenix City Story* which told a semi-fictional story of young Patterson avenging his father's assassination by cleaning up the Sin City. In newspapers, ads ran showing Patterson the clean-cut young protector of law and order. His entire advertising campaign reinforced that theme.

Wallace ran to Grover Hall. Wallace talked and Hall listened. Wallace picked Hall's brain. By the time the session ended, Wallace had a visual gimmick with which to attack Patterson.

On the stump the next day, Wallace stood in the bed of a pickup next to a four-poster with a patchwork quilt spread over the top.

Wallace made his usual speech, and everybody in the audience wondered why in the world he had a bed on stage with him.

At the end, he asked rhetorically, "Where is John Patterson?" He looked throughout the crowd. The people looked from person to person. "Where is John Patterson?" he asked louder.

"You know what they say?" he asked the people. "They say politics makes strange bedfellows." He lifted the edge of the quilt. He peeked between the covers. "Is that you down there, John Patterson? Why don't you come out and face the people? What do you have to hide, John?"

The people chattered. They laughed. He was making fun of John Patterson. The people were laughing at Patterson, which, Wallace thought, would surely bring him out in the open.

But Patterson remained silent. His radio and television advertisements doubled, but he made no personal appearances.

In the third week, the Ku Klux Klan publicly endorsed Patterson. When Wallace heard about it, he was on the phone to Grover Hall, who suggested an addition to the bed speech.

The next time Wallace raised the sheet he called out, "Who's down there between those sheets with you, John? Are you in bed with the Ku Klux Klan?" And the people howled.

In the last week Wallace asked, "Why doesn't John Patterson show himself and debate the issues? He's afraid. He's afraid of the issues because he knows nothing about the issues. He has given no one a possible program. What will he do for you? Nothing! He's a do-nothing, know-nothing, invisible candidate."

On the following Tuesday evening they were back in Hall's office. Once again Wallace was pacing the floor. Once again Hall was reading the returns. And once again Patterson was ahead — this time by some sixty-thousand votes.

55

Grover Hall was a flamboyant writer. He was a dapper dresser given to colorful ties and spun silk, tailored sport coats. Son of the Pulitzer Prize-winning editor of *The Advertiser,* he became editor of the same newspaper and won many writing awards himself.

Hall had been introduced to Wallace in 1946 by Ed Reid, the executive director of the Alabama League of Municipalities, whom both admired for his superior knowledge of state politics.

While Wallace was the consummate politician, seldom thinking of anything but how to further his career through Machiavellian schemes, Hall was a man for all seasons. An erudite dandy with a constant rosebud in his tailored lapel, Hall went home in the afternoons, donned his denims, and dug in the soil; he grew his own prize-winning roses and even dug the bed, brought in the peat moss and topsoil, and planted the roses himself that grow today off the southeast corner of the state capitol.

He did not always support George Wallace. When he found fault, he came down as hard as his pen would strike. But he always enjoyed Wallace. He was a friend. Although Hall fed Wallace information and ideas, and often guided him through rough times, Wallace was many times taken aback by Hall's sarcastic twist of humor.

At one of Hall's famous irregular Saturday morning stag brunches, Hall turned loose his parrots from their cage. Hall adored the parrots. He found them wonderfully independent and taught them ribald jokes. And he knew Wallace was frightened of the birds. When they were free, one perched on Wallace's shoulder and commenced to jabber away some high-pitched Middle English poetry. For better than a quarter-hour Wallace stood rigid in the middle of the living room and stared speechless at the multicolored bird. Finally Hall, with a snicker, extended his arm to the bird and relieved Wallace from the predicament.

In 1958 Hall talked his publisher, Richard Hudson Sr., into allowing him to support Wallace editorially, and he did so with great flourish. Other than the bed gimmick, Hall wrote anti-Klan speeches. His father, who had been a good friend of young Hall's idol, H.L. Mencken, had won the Pulitzer for his hard-hitting editorials criticizing Klan activities in the 1920s.

During the four years between the loss in 1958 and 1962, Hall and Wallace traveled together around the state. Hall became more enamoured with Wallace's belief that he had to be the spokesman for the entire South. Wallace told him, "You and I together will be able to make this nation see that it's not just the South that's so terrible. We know that the North commits the same sins against its people. But who chastises the North?"

Hall saw in Wallace an embodiment of the great Southern childhood myth of the warrior astride a great white charger doing battle for the love of the maiden. In Wallace's case the maiden was the people of Alabama first and the people of the South second — and later they saw a greater universe of Wallace supporters throughout the nation. For Hall, Wallace was Ivanhoe.

Hall had been born of a grand family, steeped in regional tradition and clothed in style and grace. Hall was realistic enough to know that political knights in the twentieth century did not come from aristocratic backgrounds. Wallace was the knight: emotional, energetic, single-minded, rough-hewn, strong, and appealing to the masses.

In 1963, after he was governor, Wallace suggested to Hall that he was planning to enter some presidential primaries. Hall stated, "Wallace, you're out of your mind!"

Later, however, Hall acquiesced and even became enthusiastic about Wallace's journeys into the foreign lands to the north.

That spring, when Wallace was invited for the first time to appear on *Meet the Press* before a national television audience, he asked Hall to accompany him.

Hall and his young assistant, Tom Johnson, later editor of *The Montgomery Independent,* went with the Governor to Washington D.C. Once in the capital city, Wallace began to ask Hall to write him "a foreign policy."

When Hall looked at his friend incredulously, Wallace said, "Those boys are going to question me about my beliefs tomorrow. They're going to want to know about what I think about things in this nation. And they're going to want to know about my foreign policy. If I'm going to run for the presidency next year I've got to have a foreign policy."

Even on Sunday morning before the show, Wallace continued to ask Hall about the foreign policy.

Finally Hall ripped a news column from the *Wall Street Journal* and said, "That's a perfect foreign policy."

Wallace read it a half-dozen times. Satisfied that he had it committed to memory, he stuffed it into his own breast pocket.

After the show Wallace strutted into the lobby, where Hall and Johnson waited. He lighted a cigar, pulled out the clipping, wadded it, and threw it into a waste can. "I don't need a foreign policy," he said. "All they wanted to know about was niggers, and I'm the expert."

In the days of the mid-sixties, Hall wrote of Wallace's "daring, dauntlessness, and imagination." Analyzing his own feelings, the editor wrote in a letter to a friend, "Part of my feeling [for Wallace] derives from love of Alabama and pride in the Kickapoo juice in the breed's blood. I can feel the same way about Hugo Black." He continued, "I have sometimes been cowardly about Wallace, but I hope on balance it can be said I refused to deny him in Montgomery or Richmond, costly as it was."

He was fired as editor of the *Advertiser* because he openly defied the policy of new management. He fought his own battle in his own private world, not seeking the advice of many of his friends. He became editorial-page editor of the Richmond *News-Leader*. Prior to the 1968 primaries he arranged an extensive interview for Wallace by a panel of the newspaper's executives. Hall advised him to tone down his rhetoric for the Virginians. Wallace later told New York *Times* columnist Tom Wicker that the group was "the most cultured, polite, well-dressed crowd I ever saw in my life and I gave 'em a real cultured talk . . . And then I forgot and called the Supreme Court a 'sorry, lousy, no-count outfit,' and you ought to have heard that cultured crowd stand up and cheer. People are about the same everywhere, and ol' Grover here keeps trying to polish me up."

Hall had too much Wallace and Alabama on his mind to make it in Richmond, and it was not long before he tired of the city and the Virginians of him. He went to Washington and wrote a syndicated column, calling himself "an Alabamian exuding Alabama nationalism" and nicknamed Wallace "Beelzebub Alabammus."

After Wallace garnered some ten percent of the national vote in the 1968 general election, Wallace and his people believed he could do it again in 1972 as a Democrat. They had a great deal of money. Their fund-raising ability was phenomenal.

Wallace offered his old friend a job in Montgomery as "resident intellectual" to edit *The Wallace Letter,* which was published periodically for the supporters, to write a book extolling Wallace as a national hero, to continue to write a syndicated column, and to develop radio and television material which would boost the campaign.

Troubled by fainting spells and nervous seizures, Hall prepared to leave Washington. His final column, entitled "Peck's Bad Boy," linked South Vietnamese Vice-President Ky and the Reverend Carl McIntyre. Hall delivered it to Western Union on the night of September 9, 1970, but Teletype operators found the material impossible to decipher. At least three typewritten pages were badly garbled. Hall attempted to correct the copy, but the column was never sent to the home office of Publishers-Hall Syndicate.

Hall drove out of Washington, but a week later he still had not shown up in Montgomery, where he had been scheduled to make a return-home-victorious speech to the Kiwanis Club.

Wallace, worried about his friend's disappearance, put out a missing-persons report through the Alabama state troopers, who notified all states between Alabama and the District of Columbia.

At the end of two weeks he still had not shown.

It was later learned that he had apparently spent the first week traveling southward very slowly through Virginia and North Carolina. On the eighth day he was stopped by a Mecklenburg County, North Carolina, policeman at 2:45 a.m. near Charlotte.

He had alcohol on his breath and a half-bottle of Scotch on the front seat.

The officer arrested Hall and charged him with driving while under the influence of alcohol. He was given a breath test when he was jailed. It showed he did not have enough alcohol in his system to make him drunk. Nevertheless, he was arrested on a second charge of driving without a license.

During the next seven days the fifty-year-old journalist was confined to the county jail, until a supervisor notified a medical official that Hall needed treatment.

The official, trained in first aid, examined Hall and told the jailer to watch for symptoms of alcoholic withdrawal.

On the following day, after Hall had not complained once of feeling badly, the jailer said Hall claimed to be a newspaper writer.

An editor at the Charlotte *Observer* was notified, went to the jail, recognized Hall, who was then taken to Memorial Hospital, where it was determined that he had suffered a brain tumor. His condition worsened quickly.

A special ambulance airplane transferred him to Birmingham's University Hospital, where he underwent surgery for a cystic tumor in the right frontal area of the brain. It was highly malignant, and he remained in the Birmingham hospital to undergo cobalt treatment.

Wheelchair-ridden, he came home to Montgomery to a quaint tree-shaded home in the gracious Old Cloverdale district. As wryly humorous as ever, he made the best of a terrible physical situation, and among his frequent callers were Wallace and his new bride, the former Cornelia Ellis Snively, whom Hall proposed to be the cover girl of a new Wallace brochure. He also suggested that Cornelia pose in a red velvet gown, and whenever the Wallaces visited, he asked them to hurry with the project. But it was never completed.

Exactly one year after he had been found in the jail, Hall died. *The New York Times* eulogized the 1957 Headliner Award winner as "probing, wry, and capable of great courage." Wallace stated, "We have lost one of the finest journalists Alabama has ever produced."

In a time when the poetry leaked from his pen with great meaning, Grover Hall wrote of Montgomery: "We love our city here in the bend of a yellow river. We venerate its famous past. We cherish the style and individuality of the present. And, we trust not vaingloriously, the city's sunburst future we take for granted, even though it may mean a bit of factory soot on the magnolia blossoms.

"As is the case with highly endowed individuals, the city's personality is complex; it sometimes baffles newcomers, sometimes frustrates them. One aspect of its personality is that it is imbued with a kind of sophistication that refuses to be bowled over by any grandee, magnifico, potentate or man-made event. The city's past as a national capital is one of the reasons its eyes never pop."

A Lawyer For Rich Or Poor

Charles Morgan Jr. was tired.

For the two nights prior to this day in court, he and his associates had been working to put together the final pieces of the complicated lawsuit.

Now, at the end of a long day, Morgan stood with heavy slumped shoulders, leaning against a knotted cane.

His sparkling liquid green eyes stared up into the stern face of U.S. District Judge Frank M. Johnson Jr., a friend whom Morgan would later call "the greatest judge in the United States."

Morgan had finished arguing the case for his clients, a group of poor black people from south and central Alabama. Now, Johnson said, he wanted written briefs prepared and delivered to his office by the following morning.

"But, your honor," Morgan began in his booming baritone. He chronicled his long and hard hours of work that had led up to the court appearance. And he added that he had undergone surgery on his leg only several months earlier.

"Mr. Morgan," Johnson cajoled at the end of the lawyer's plea, "you love this hard work. Now, I'll need the brief by tomorrow morning."

Grumbling, Morgan hobbled out of the courthouse in Montgomery and within an hour was esconced in his nearby motel room, lawbooks stacked around him, a telephone in each hand, a bottle of bourbon between his knees, and wearing only a pair of baggy undershorts.

By eight the next morning a freshly written and typed brief was delivered by Morgan to Judge Johnson.

Morgan always grumbled. He enjoyed grumbling just as he loved the courtroom. "Out of more than 31,000 lawyers in Washington, D.C., only a little more than a thousand have ever had trial experience. Can you believe that?" Morgan half shouted. The inflection in his voice gave the words an incredible and incredulous twist. "I would be ashamed if I didn't march into a courtroom before I was a year out of law school."

Charles Morgan Jr., born in Kentucky and raised on the north Alabama mountain outside Birmingham overlooking the steel mills in the distance, developed a sense of drama. He admired the dramatic action of a trial, and even if he lost a case, he talked about it as though he had been victorious; because, by God, he had been there!

Since his days at the University of Alabama in Tuscaloosa he championed civil rights. During those days he tried to help Autherine Lucy, the first black to attempt to integrate the state school in the early 1950s. And from that time he carried the banner for Dr. Martin Luther King Jr., Muhammad Ali, students in trouble, and soldiers who refused to carry out orders to kill civilians in Vietnam. However, in recent years he caught the blunt of criticism from many who once held him in esteem as their legal savior because he chose to represent big-money establishment clients such as Sears, Roebuck & Company, North Carolina university system, and others.

In private practice for the first time since the early 1960s in what he called "high-cotton offices" on L Street Northwest in downtown Washington, he represented Sears in a suit which frightened civil rights groups because it challenged the federal government's authority to force private companies to hire minorities. Morgan claimed that the government was wishy-washy in its everpresent guidelines.

Armed with boxes filled with statistics, Morgan declared in the suit that white males have had the greatest benefits from government hiring policies from veterans' preferences following World War II. In the Sears suit, termed "the most massive corporate assault to date on federal regulations," Morgan maintained that the federal retirement deadline extension further benefited white males. "The white men who received the veterans' preferences were the same ones gaining from last year's extension," he said.

His loud voice resounded through his renovated house on Capitol Hill, "A reporter asked me the other day, 'Do corporations have civil rights?'" His laughter shook his massive Hemingwayesque chest. "I said, 'Yes, indeed, corporations certainly do have civil rights. They too are protected under the Constitution of these United States.'" He laughed again. "They just don't seem to understand that Sears has been discriminated against by a bureaucracy that can't make up its mind from week to week what sort of preference it wants to give to *whom!*" The last word jolted an octave higher. "First, the government bureaucracy, which is the new American upper-class — government employees — the top level of the fifteen to twenty percent of our employed citizens who live off taxes extracted from their fellow citizens, cannot make up its mind from week to week who receives the hiring preferences. They hand down new guidelines, changed from last week's guidelines."

Even in the comfort of his own living room with an audience of one, Morgan could not help but argue his point dramatically. "The bureaucracy works closely with our liberal community which is salaried from tax deductible and foundation funds and draws upon inherited wealth in the public interest.

"Long before benign liberalism kills capitalism, it will have so crippled it that it will knuckle under the sheer weight of nonproductive bureaucracy. To survive, all economic systems must produce something of value, of quality, of need. Yet in the city where I now live — one of the world's largest company towns — the number one manufacturing industry is printing. It is a do-nothing, produce-nothing society."

After the Sears suit was thrown out of U.S. District Court in Washington for being "frivolous," Morgan and his associates appealed. In a mammouth trial in Chicago, after a season in court, he won the case for Sears. He was adamant in his absolute belief that his client never did and never intended to violate the rights of black or white female employees.

Other than the pure cutting edge sharpness of his brain power, Morgan's long suit was always his never-say-quit persistence. For years and years he worked with a case to reapportion the Alabama State Legislature. He was defeated on the first level. But he continued to appeal, until one person, one vote was made the law of the land by the U.S. Supreme Court. That case alone, stating that each person had a right to be represented not simply by county lines, revolutionized local elections. And when a young black elected to the Georgia House of Representatives was denied the oath of office, Morgan stood up for him against the claim that he had supported a statement against Americans fighting in Vietnam. After Morgan battled in courtrooms from Atlanta to Washington, Julian Bond was given the seat he had won.

Representing the university system of North Carolina in a suit brought by the Department of Health, Education, and Welfare, Morgan again saw his old friends raise their eyebrows in his direction. What on earth, they said, is he trying to do? If he lost the case, the first southern schools to desegregate would become the first to lose federal funding because it would not comply with certain regulations.

"They point their accusing finger at North Carolina," said Morgan. In U.S. District Court in Raleigh, Morgan pointed out that North Carolina had "a higher level of desegregation than most other institutions of high education North and South." He said that the Department of HEW "is singling out the South as the whipping boy." He showed that during the previous year, North Carolina's predominantly white campuses had a greater percentage of black students than Harvard. North Carolina had six percent, Harvard 5.2, and in North Carolina's professional programs, medicine and law, blacks totaled more than nine percent.

But the problem appeared to be the $40 million slated to be spent for new academic programs and buildings at five of the state's predominantly black campuses, where at least seventy percent of the state's 20,500 black students were enrolled. The government insisted that more white students be made to attend these schools to even the ratio in all the state's universities.

Sociologists said that if the black students were forced to attend the predominantly white schools, sixty-eight percent would not go to college, Morgan stated.

When his old friends criticized his motives, Morgan shook his head. "I give my clients their money's worth," he said. He would not apologize for his most recent cases.

"I do not understand why all the liberals are jumping on Chuck Morgan," allowed one of his friends from New York. "Here again, Chuck is fighting big government. He has been doing that all of his life. Now he has to fight harder. He is over fifty years old. Back when he was fighting the racists and the Ku Klux Klan in Alabama, it was easier to see. Today, he is fighting for the same principles."

Morgan told a gathering of well-heeled backers of the American Civil Liberties Union, for whom he worked in Atlanta and Washington for more than fifteen years, "Early in life, I decided I wanted to be a lawyer. Not a corporation lawyer, not a political lawyer, not a constitutional lawyer, not a civil liberties lawyer, not a civil rights lawyer, not a criminal lawyer, but just a lawyer.

"As a lawyer, I knew there were many publics and many interests. Lately I have read a few malign messages from liberals who, while less gutteral, now send the messages I previously received from the likes of Birmingham's Police Commissioner T. Eugene 'Bull' Connor. Like the Connors and J. Edgar Hoovers of yesterday, these liberals presume certain of my clients guilty."

Back in Birmingham Morgan fought with all his might against the Connor-style government. One of his first cases, after he finished law school at the University of Alabama with honors, was as court-appointed attorney for a poor black man suffering from heart and lung ailments. "That was back when the courts of Alabama paid lawyers $100 for indigent cases — including research expenses," Morgan recalled.

The man, Henry Williams, was accused of killing a poor paralyzed widow, mother of four, by beating her with a gun barrel.

Morgan searched through the rundown shacks of the Negro quarters of north Birmingham until he finally found a witness who told him his client had been living with the widow for months. Questioning the witness closer, Morgan learned that the woman had laughed, made fun of Henry Williams, and hugged another man in front of him.

As Henry Williams sat on the porch of his shack, he watched the woman carrying on. She told the crowd, "He ain't no good as a man no mo'," the witness said.

"With the cackle of laughter in his ears, Henry picked up a gun barrel lying on the ground and swung. In that elemental world in which he was dying, Henry, who couldn't work or read or write or even talk, he had been revealed to all as being impotent. And so he killed her," Morgan remembered.

His client was not set free. A few years later he died of natural causes in prison.

Since those days of the long, hot, civil rights summers, Morgan remained in his home town and fought against the oppressers, defending black and white workers in hostile courtrooms. As far back as 1961, he filed the one man, one vote reapportionment case in U.S. District Court in Montgomery while the Alabama Legislature was in session. "In those days, lobbyists came to Montgomery with a suitcase full of whiskey to win friends and votes.

"We decided it was time to take some of the power away from the Big Mules — former Alabama Governor Big Jim Folsom's name for the big-moneyed powers (U.S. Steel in Birmingham, Alabama Power Company and others) — and we knew we had to do it in court."

The case was stymied for a while. But it climbed up through the court system with Morgan's persistence. Before he stepped down from the longest tenure on the U.S. Supreme Court, Justice William O. Douglas was asked which case "had the most impact on the country and its citizens." After thinking a few minutes, he replied, "*Reynolds v. Sims,* "the reapportionment case which made one person, one vote the law.

Visiting reporters in Birmingham used to tease Morgan about looking like a deputy sheriff, and he always shrugged his heavy shoulders and said he had to look like them to keep from being killed by them.

He continued to speak out in court and out of court. Perhaps his most memorable time on the soap box came after four little black girls were killed in the bombing of the Sixteenth Street Baptist Church in Birmingham in September of 1963. He stood stoop-shouldered and heavy-jowled before the all-white Young Men's Business Club and pointed his finger in their faces.

"Four little girls were killed in Birmingham yesterday," his voice rang out. "A mad, remorseful, worried community asks, 'Who did it? Who threw that bomb? Was it a Negro or a white?' The answer should be, 'We all did it.' Every last one of us is condemned for that crime and the bombing before it and the ones last month, last year, a decade ago. We all did it," he said.

He accused the city of not having politicians who would stand up against bigotry. He stated that Birmingham had no black policemen, and a racist police commissioner who didn't care. He said most of the white ministers turned their backs on violence

66

against blacks. And he added that the city had a moderate mayor who moved too slowly.

Shortly after this powerful speech, his law practice dwindled to nothing. Telephone threats became a way of life. Finally, he, his wife Camille, a native of Birmingham, and their son, Charles, moved to Virginia. Morgan worked for the American Association of University Professors and later the NAACP Defense Fund while he wrote his first autobiographical book, *A Time To Speak*.

When he was offered the regional directorship of the ACLU in Atlanta, Morgan jumped at the chance to get back into the thick of the civil rights struggle. Like a southbound tornado, Morgan moved into the offices at Five Forsythe Street which became a mecca for students, newsmen, black and white politicians who were fighting George Wallace-like racist grandstanding, and northern professors who were traveling through Dixie. "Unfortunately most of them were summer soldiers who came South and then went back home," he said while lounging in the sun behind his vacation home on Choctawhatchee Bay in the Florida panhandle fishing village of Destin. "They didn't understand what the fight was all about," he added.

He knew what the fight was about. He winged his way from one end of the South to the other, filing suits to desegregate jury lists, to include women on Alabama juries, to desegregate prison systems and to stop white officials from omitting black political candidates' names on ballots.

Like a heavyweight on a white horse, he was in and out of dozens of military bases throughout the South, defending anti-war demonstrators, religious groups who came to pray for peace, and other protesters.

When he defended Captain Howard Levy on charges of refusing to train medical personnel to kill with medicine during the Vietnam War, Morgan put the military on trial. He argued loudly and eloquently.

Through testimony, Morgan showed that even the agent who had first informed on Levy knew little about Constitutional principles; he was against someone who would not teach medical men to kill. And when Morgan got expert witness, best-selling novelist Robin Moore on the stand, he asked, "What is an assassination team?"

Reporters made frantic notes when the author of *The Green Berets* testified, "It's a team trained to hit targets, a target being the term generally used for an individual to be assassinated for political reasons or whatever. It is an integral part of guerrilla warfare just as is medical people trying to help people of an area to win the hearts and minds of the people. An assassination is also an important aspect."

At the end of Morgan's final argument, veteran New York *Times* reporter Homer Bigart's wife, Alice, told the lawyer, "He could never tell you himself, but I can. To us you are the Beethoven of the legal profession."

Nevertheless, the officers found Levy guilty, sentenced him to three years hard labor, and Morgan persisted until the U.S. Supreme Court reversed the case.

The Vietnam War also brought him another case which was to become famous.

When Muhammad Ali made his conscientious objector claim, he hired Morgan. With the lawyer at his side, Ali told the government's hearing officer, "When I go in a ring, my intentions [sic] is not to be violent in the way of fighting to kill, or going to war, or hurting no one physically; it's not my faith, and we have a referee in the ring, and I'm known as a scientific fighter and as a fast, classy boxer, and we have three judges and we have an ambulance and we have doctors and we are not one nation against another or one race against another or one religion against another. It's just the art of boxing . . ."

When the Justice Department's own hearing officer ruled that Ali was sincere in his beliefs, the government overruled their own man.

In court, Morgan defended Ali and discovered along the way that Robert F. Kennedy as attorney general had approved wiretaps of Dr. Martin Luther King Jr.'s telephone.

"The headlines from that discovery alone were enough to push anti-war sentiment to an all-time high," he said. "I pushed it for all it was worth. Isn't that what a lawyer should do?" he said with head-tilted audacity, his full lips twisted into a sarcastic grin.

"In every case that I fought I did so against great odds. I was not jumping out in front of the pack with a favorite cause. I was pushing against the grain. I was fighting the powers that be. And many, many people presumed my clients guilty before they had one day in court."

He was not only a tough courtroom warrior, he held his own in the barrooms across the southland with hard-drinking journalists and fellow lawyers. When he heard of the death of his friend, Dr. King, he ordered a fifth of whiskey and drank it and cried. And he knows the exact day more than three years later — June 13, 1971 — when he quit drinking, and he has not touched a drop since. In fact, he became so adamant against it, his friends have teased, that he threatened to sue airlines if there was wine in desserts served to him. Then he popped, "You're damn right I'm serious!"

In 1971, he was offered the directorship of the national ACLU office in Washington. "It was time to move on," he said. "You can't stay in one spot too long. You grow stale."

From the national office, he defended not only poor blacks, anti-war demonstrators, conscientious objectors, but also the Ku Klux Klan when they were refused the right to march. "Every person and organization in this country deserves the best legal representation possible. I don't care who they are or what they are."

When Watergate first became a national issue, Morgan stepped in from the sidelines and represented the Association of State Democratic Chairmen, the office of which had been burglarized.

In his most recent autobiographical volume, *One Man, One Voice,* Morgan outlined his major cases since Birmingham with emphasis on Watergate.

"In the Watergate case, conduct, not associations and beliefs, was at issue. So was fear," he wrote, comparing it to the early 1950s when Senator Joe McCarthy was frightening the country with his anti-Communist witch hunt.

"In Birmingham, we chose sides. In Washington, there were no sides. The blandest led the bland and the word controversial was as frightening as the word partisan.

"Washington was worse than a company town. It was a gigantic firm," he wrote.

Throughout Watergate, Morgan pushed for the impeachment of President Nixon. "People didn't realize what impeach means," he said. "They thought if he was impeached, he was automatically guilty. That was not and is not the case. I wanted to see Nixon brought before the tribunal with the best of legal representation and tried before the nation; that is impeachment."

He never let up in his courtroom work for the ACLU, in his fund-raising and his membership drives. But he parted ways with the organization after he overheard a New York representative of ACLU make the statement that he could never vote for a southern governor for President. Morgan, who had known Jimmy Carter when he was governor of Georgia, turned to the man and said, "That's bigotry." And anyone who knew Morgan realized that he had never stopped with the utterance of only two words.

When Roy Reed, a national correspondent for *The New York Times,* heard the story he telephoned Morgan for confirmation. Morgan said it was true and that furthermore the northern establishment liberals were against Carter because they didn't "have their hooks in him" and they're afraid they "won't have access if he's elected."

After the article appeared, ACLU Executive Director Aryeh Neier contacted Morgan and asked what steps he was taking to correct the impression that he was speaking for the organization. Morgan replied, "The step I am taking is to resign."

With Camille as his secretary, he ventured into the world of private law. "And since then we have both loved it," Camille said in a pleasant sing-song Southern voice. "It's not everybody who can start over again. We're having a great time. We have the courage to do it. I can't help but think that some people are showing their sour grapes when they criticize Chuck."

And it was obvious, watching them talk about it, that it did hurt when they heard about an old friend questioning Chuck's motives.

"Who do they think I am?" he asked rhetorically as he leaned back in the lounging chair behind the neat little home where he spent most of each summer. "To those who ask, 'Has Chuck Morgan sold out?' I say, 'Chuck Morgan never sold in.'"

"It is my duty and my pleasure to serve my client's cause. As Clarence Darrow said when representing a wealthy defendant, 'I do not believe I need to tell this court, or my friends, that I would fight just as hard for the poor as for the rich.'"

Chuck Morgan was determined to continue fighting. He argued in Virginia in behalf of a sixty-one-year-old coffee shop owner who

70

insisted that she had a Constitutional right to allow her customers to smoke in her place of business.

"We raised the question that she has given the public sufficient notice with a three-inch sign on her door stating SMOKING PERMITTED just above No Sleeveless T-shirts and No Bare Feet," Morgan said between puffs of his cigarette.

"We are saying that she is placing people on sufficient notice when there is no specific law against smoking. This is a First Amendment case of free speech, free association. Here we have raised the right of commercial association."

He grinned as smoke rushed up his face. "I'll probably have the consumer people against me on this one. But I think little of the consumer programs. They're a bunch of people wanting to put the Good Housekeeping seal of approval on life."

Closing his eyes, he spoke of the "Dom Perignon liberals who jog in lock-step, order white wine, cluck about Coca-Colas and present themselves as representatives of the common wealth." While the waves of the Choctawhatchee Bay beat rhythmically against the nearby seawall, he quoted a speech he gave in Chicago, "The ancestors of blacks, unlike the ancestors of the rest of us, did not come to this land of their own free will. They will, however, be freed from the vestiges of slavery only by the free exercise of their own will. It is in the nature of government, even benignly liberal governments, to oppress. It is in the nature of a free people to resist." And he echoed the poet James Oppenheim, "Free men set themselves free." He grinned widely and raised his glass of ice water.

A Funny, Angry Man

In the fall of 1968 I wrote a series of articles about the prevalence of illegal drugs among the young people of Alabama. Published for eight straight days in *The Alabama Journal,* these pieces disrupted a few minds — especially in the capital city, where I had actually purchased a cigarette of marijuana at a downtown establishment within three blocks of the newspaper offices.

I was immediately called before the grand jury meeting at the county courthouse. I was confronted by an irate district attorney, who asked me to reveal the names of all the people who had been quoted in my stories. I told him that I had given my word I would not reveal their names, that these sources were privileged under Alabama law, and a circuit judge threatened me with jail if I did not tell the names. *Journal-Advertiser* publisher Harold Martin, who later won a Pulitzer Prize for his own investigations into illegal activities within the State Department of Corrections, told the DA, the judge and the jury that he stood behind me and my stories one-hundred percent.

Of course, there were stories on the television that night about my refusing to identify my sources. On the following morning I was contacted by a young man who said he and his friends would like to meet me and would like to tell me about drug activity in Montgomery schools.

There was a catch, however, to their talking: I had to promise to keep their identities secret. I agreed.

I met with six young men and women at a local restaurant in the open. Any number of persons saw us talking. These were sons and daughters of prominent citizens of the city.

73

They told about junior high school children who began taking pills, smoking marijuana, and using other drugs. They told about high school students who smoked marijuana in the rest rooms of their schools between classes. They told about young people who stole money from their parents to buy drugs. They told about some who sold the drugs to pay for their own habits.

On the following afternoon, their stories were printed in *The Journal*. An hour later a deputy sheriff showed up with a subpoena. I was summoned before the grand jury immediately.

Publisher Martin and I walked across the street. We stood before the jury. Again I told them I had promised anonymity. Again the DA threatened me with jail. Again I said I could not give them the names.

After questioning me for several hours, we were told by an editor that one of the young people had called the office. They had heard I was in trouble. They said they would come forth and testify before the grand jury, if the DA would promise not to reveal their identities.

Red-faced, the DA half-screamed, "If they come here, I'll give 'em what they deserve: jail!"

When I looked out at the grand jurors, I saw they were astonished. They knew they would never receive the truth from the young people who had drug problems or knew of drug problems. Instead, the DA paraded a group of student leaders who said they knew of no drug problems whatsoever in the schools.

As a result of the turmoil created by the series of articles, *The Journal* called for the creation of a committee to study the drug problems in Montgomery's schools. I was appointed to the committee, chaired by YMCA Executive Director Bill Chandler, and we made a report which reiterated the problems which my stories had originally pointed out. We made speeches in local schools and to civic clubs. Within the next year my series won a number of journalism awards, including the prestigious Associated Press National Managing Editors Award.

The most important thing that came from the series for me personally was an introduction to a person who turned out to be one of the most stubbornly irascible, blatantly honest, tenaciously intelligent, and frighteningly sarcastic individuals I have ever known in my life. A man with a grating sort of raspy voice called the newspaper office, said he'd like to buy my lunch and some beers would be thrown in, and "all I want to know is everything you know about cannabis saliva."

"What the hell do you want to know about marijuana for?" I asked.

"I'm a lawyer. I've got four young clients. The oldest is twenty-one. They're all students at Troy State College. They're being charged with possession of cannabis or marijuana. Investigators found less than one teaspoonful and now these kids are facing the possibility — the *strong* possibility — of five years in state prison."

"When do you want to meet?" I asked.

"What's wrong with now?" he said.

I met him at Joe's Delicatessen, a great old Cloverdale institution operated by Joe Piha until his death in the early 1980s.

George W. Dean Jr. had been born not far from the delicatessen forty-some-odd years earlier, had been raised a maverick on these suburban streets, and had never been comfortable being just another lawyer. He always sought intellectual and social challenges in his work, and this was no different.

We nibbled pastrami sandwiches, sipped beer, and I heard about his quartet of clients. The Alabama State Department of Public Safety investigators had gone undercover, discovered marijuana trafficking on the Troy campus some fifty miles south of Montgomery, and by scraping the insides of the four students' chests-of-drawers were able to come up with a total of less than one teaspoonful of illegal substance.

I told George about my experiences around the state, he told me about being involved in civil rights litigation and assisting Chuck Morgan with ACLU cases, and before we knew it the late afternoon beer-drinking crowd had descended upon us.

That was the beginning of a long friendship which I still hold dear. My editors agreed to my covering the trial of Dean's clients. For the first time since the late 1930s someone was being tried under the law which gave the judge in the case no discretionary authority. If the young men were found guilty of possession of marijuana, the judge was required by statute to sentence the defendants to five years in state prison.

First, the administration of Troy State expelled the students as soon as they were indicted. Dean asked for a hearing, saying his clients were being denied their rights under the Constitution. He was turned down. He went into U.S. Court in Montgomery, appeared before District Judge Frank M. Johnson Jr., who agreed with Dean's interpretation of the law.

A hearing was scheduled, the participants entered the room, but school authorities closed the door in my face when I started to enter. "This is a private hearing," I was told. Dean protested.

Again Dean carried the case before Judge Johnson, and again Johnson ruled in his favor. He said the hearing must be open to the public. The school's attorney protested, saying I had written untrue stories concerning the defendants and the school. Johnson said that he found my articles true "per se," and I swelled with pride. I had never received a higher compliment from someone I knew was a great jurist.*

After the hearing, the four young men were again expelled. Then they were tried by twelve men and women who heard the evidence that stated emphatically that marijuana had been found in the bottom of their chests-of-drawers.

"How did you discover this marijuana?" Dean asked the investigator.

"We were told by a reliable witness that these young men had smoked marijuana. We followed through on that lead and obtained a search warrant and searched their room."

"Did you see the marijuana laying out on a chest?" Dean asked.

"No, sir," he replied.

"Where'd you find it? Laying inside a drawer?"

"Kind of," he said.

"How 'kind of'?" he asked.

"Well, it was inside a drawer."

"In a sack?"

"No, sir."

"In a plastic container the way it is now, lying here on this table?"

"No, sir."

"How'd you find it?"

"It was on the bottom of a drawer."

"How'd you get it?"

"We just got it up."

"How? With a knife?"

---

*Some sixteen years later, Troy State University honored me with their highest journalistic award. I was given the Hector Award for outstanding performance in journalism and the Grover Cleveland Hall Jr. Fellowship.

The prosecution objected to Dean's leading the witness. But Judge Eris Paul, a tall, white-haired, soft-voiced gentleman, said, "Let the witness answer."

"How did you retrieve the marijuana?" Dean asked. "Did you scrape it up?"

"Yes, sir."

"With a knife?"

"Yes, sir."

"You took a knife and scraped up little-bitty pieces, did you not?"

"Yes, sir, we did."

"You couldn't hardly see it, could you?"

Again the prosecution objected, and this time the judge sustained.

But Dean had made his point.

When the jurors came in with their decision, three of the women were in tears. They found the young men guilty.

Judge Paul called Dean to the bench. "I don't have to tell you what you need to do right after I do what I have to do under the law."

Dean nodded. "No, sir, your honor. I know."

After the judge sentenced each of the young men to five years, Dean drove quickly to Montgomery, went into District Court, and obtained a temporary restraining order setting aside the verdict and the sentence until all federal appeals were exhausted.

Ultimately, three of the defendants served more than one year in state prison. The fourth went back to his home in New Jersey and later crossed into Canada. After several years of appeals, Morris Dees and the Southern Poverty Law Center took up the case and had it reversed on the grounds of a faulty search.

In the meantime, George Dean continued legal fights for student rights that started with the marijuana cases. When a group of students took over Flowers Hall at Tuskegee Institute, the young blacks were arrested, charged with misdemeanors, and promptly expelled from school. Dean was their legal champion in court, won for them their reinstatement as students, and all but one was vindicated in court.

Several years later, when the students at the University of Alabama staged an afternoon of anti-Vietnam War speeches and an evening of candlelight vigils in memory of the students killed at

Kent State for protesting the war, Dean accompanied me to the campus. While I covered the events for *The Journal,* Dean talked with a number of students and professors involved in the more-or-less subtle happenings on the campus. There had been a number of protests, the most violent of which was the burning of an old ROTC building which had not been used in years. We grabbed a bit of early dinner and headed south toward Montgomery at twilight. Several miles out of town, Dean said, "Why the hell would any protesters burn a building no longer in use? If you were a protester and wanted to make a point, wouldn't you burn something useful and meaningful?" I drove along, saying nothing. After a few minutes, Dean said, "You think they might be doing something back at the campus?" I didn't even question him once. I turned around and headed back. As we drove slowly down sorority row, several city buses pulled into the parking lot behind the Student Union Building. Several hundred students lined University Avenue in front of the Union Building. I parked quickly and we got out.

We inched through the crowd toward demonstrators. We saw that pro-President Nixon students held signs on the steps of the Union Building while anti-war demonstrators showed signs diagonally across the avenue at the corner of the Quadrangle. Behind us, we saw uniformed city policemen stepping off the buses. Armed with billyclubs, they moved into the middle of the street, forming a wall between the students. I saw that the police had on their badges but their numbers were covered with black tape. As I moved close to a policeman, I identified myself and told him I was with *The Alabama Journal.* He pushed the stick toward me, holding it in both hands in front of his chest. "I don't care who you are, get back on the curb!"

"I need to get to the public telephone under the steps," I said.

He shook his head and held his stick in front of me.

At that instant, the scream from the mouth of a female student pierced the air.

I looked around.

Behind the line of police, another uniformed man pulled a young woman across the asphalt by the hair. In her hands was a sign that read: We Support Nixon.

A moment later another woman screamed. It was a blood-curdling sound.

All of a sudden, the line of police broke. They moved helter-skelter. I heard a grunt next to me. Thinking it was Dean, I looked. It was a man in a dark suit. A policeman had hit him across the elbow, which he was holding.

I broke for the Union Building. I ducked under the steps, dropped a quarter in the phone, dialed my number, and told City Editor John Williams of *The Montgomery Advertiser*, "All hell's breaking loose up here! The cops have gone mad!"

A policeman headed my way. He pulled back his billystick and swung it toward me. I dropped the receiver, ducked my head, and ran.

As I scurried up the hill toward the first fraternity house beyond the Union Building, a club hit the back of my leg. I moved faster. Out of breath, I rushed through the front door of the house. I told the frantic students who I was, they led me to an upstairs room, gave me a telephone, and I got an open line to Editor Williams. He turned me over to Executive Managing Editor Ben Davis, who had been my first boss as city editor of the *Tuscaloosa News* when I was only fifteen years old. "It's the damndest thing thing I've ever seen," I said. I described what I had seen happening and what I was currently seeing from the second-floor window. It was difficult for him to believe, but after several minutes, he said, "We're turning you over to a secretary. Talk fast and accurately. Afterwards, we'll read it back. For heaven's sake, don't get off the phone." So I began. The students who had been chased into the building by policemen were rushed up the stairs. They gave me their names and home towns and told what they had been doing when the police attacked. They paraded through — a pretty young woman from Bay Minette who had been out for a walk with her date, a KA who had been on his way to pick up his date at the Tri-Delt house, a young man who had dropped and lost his books — making a whale of a story.

After I finished and after the storm died, I went out to look for my friend George Dean. I discovered him on the far side of University Avenue, sitting on the steps of the University Police headquarters. He said he'd gone there looking for me.

As it turned out, more than fifty students were arrested, hauled off to jail in the city buses which had brought the police to the campus.

At the home of Jay and Alberta Murphy, an individualistic and iconoclastic law professor and his individualistic and iconoclastic lawyer wife, we heard more tales of what had happened to whom. It was decided by one of the campus leaders that George would defend the students. George and local attorney, Jack Drake, who had been president of the University's Student Government Association several years before, decided they would ask City Judge Joe Burn to allow the students to be freed on their own recognizance.

By the time an affidavit was drawn up for the judge to sign it was past midnight.

"Don't you think we should call first?" asked Drake.

"Let's just take it to him. We don't want to give him a chance to say no," Dean said.

I rode with them. At the white frame house near Tuscaloosa County Club all was quiet and dark. Dean stepped onto the small front stoop. Drake was behind Dean, and I was behind Drake.

Dean rapped loudly on the front door.

When no one answered the knock, Dean rapped louder.

From inside, a gruff voice said, "Who the hell is it?"

"This is George W. Dean Jr., your honor. I'm a lawyer. I've got a paper for you to sign."

"At this time of night?"

"Yes, sir. You see, sir, there're fifty students from the University in the city jail, and we'd like you to let them out."

We heard movement from the other side of the door and the voice said, "Mama, give me my gun, there's some crazy people out here."

Drake and I moved back into the darkness.

Dean held his place. "Your honor, I'd like you to take a look at this paper."

"I'm denying whatever request you've got. I suggest you come to my office tomorrow morning."

"This morning, your honor?" Dean asked.

"Hell, yes, this morning! Now, get!"

Back at the Murphys' house, Dean began calling friends to collect bond money. At one hundred dollars each, the total came to little more than five thousand.

A number of Tuscaloosa County property owners agreed to

sign bonds, but by nine a.m., Judge Burns had agreed to allow the students to sign their own bonds.

As they came out of jail Dean met with them. He would defend them free of charge if they wished.

I met them outside, talked with each, discovered their activities of the previous night, and wrote my story standing next to my car.

By noon I telephoned my story to *The Journal.* City Editor Joe McFadden said, "This is a weird one. *The Advertiser* had a banner across page one with your story this morning. Nobody else in the state got the story."

No other reporter had been present when the police had gone on the rampage. Other news organizations across the state were being handfed "facts" from the office of University President David Matthews. It was being called "a student riot."

That afternoon Dean and I finally found beds at the home of the Murphys. We slept three or four hours, awakened, Dean talked with more of his clients, and I did a follow-up.

On the next morning Matthews walked from fraternity to fraternity to apologize to the members for "the ill-advised happenings of the night before." But when he stood in the living room of the KA house, the members booed him. At another house he was told, "If you had listened, this would not happen. When are you going to begin listening to students?"

As police accompanied Matthews down sorority row, girls poked their heads from windows and shouted in decidedly southern accents, "Pigs! Pigs!"

In several of the sorority houses Matthews was again booed and he was again criticized for being "too private in your presidency." And one young woman said, "You should be out there talking to the kids who were arrested and hurt last night. You should be telling them you're sorry."

By the following day hearings for fifty-three students were set, other arrangements were being made for hearing officer, and the prosecution was preparing its cases.

I returned to Montgomery to discover that we were still the only news outlet in the state which had dared to print the student side of the story. Publisher Martin and Editor Ray Jenkins and City Editor McFadden said we needed a long first-person story. "Just sit down and write it all out, just like it happened to you," said Jenkins. "We'll put it on page one Sunday," Martin said.

I was dog-tired. I had had little more than two or three hours sleep each night. I was trying to stay up with Dean, and I wanted to know everything I could find out about the student leadership and what had happened in the aftermath of the Kent State situation where several young students were shot and killed by Ohio National Guardsmen during student demonstrations on that campus.

Somebody had firebombed the old ROTC building. The student leaders didn't know who. I talked to several dozen students but could find out little.

I also had attempted to discover what had been happening in President Matthews' office. Some of my old friends from the news media now worked for Matthews, and I saw pained expressions on their faces when I asked them about activities there. I knew they had been ordered not to talk, but I couldn't write that. Several told me in subsequent months that they had orders to keep quiet.

I wrote the story in simple one, two, three, four fashion, just as it had occurred in front of me from the moments that Wednesday afternoon when the young men and women stood in the shadows of Denny Chimes and made their anti-war speeches.

The story ended with my talking with a young man from Minnesota who worked as a milkman early in the mornings to put himself through school at the University of Alabama. He told about how he had been on the fringe of the unrest and had been caught up in the police strike on the campus that Wednesday night.

I went back to Tuscaloosa the following week, met with Dean at the Murphys' house, learned that he suspected FBI and possibly even CIA undercover work, and he said, "You know, it's a wonder that all these kids weren't killed instead of rounded up and put in jail."

When I met with students, dozens came up to me and thanked me for the articles I had written. "Our parents said that's the only way they could know we were telling the truth when we told them what was happening down here," was the refrain.

Late that afternoon New York Congressman Allard Lowenstein, conducting informal hearings around the U.S. on student problems, held an open forum in an auditorium in the basement of the Student Union Building. It was packed.

After Lowenstein opened the meeting by telling his intentions of "trying to discover the truth of what is happening on our campuses," Dean rose.

In jeans and sweatshirt — clothing purchased after he stayed in Tuscaloosa with only the clothes on his back — he opened his arms to them and grinned his silly-faced ear-to-ear grin. "Many of you are my clients," he said softly. "Others of you are my friends. I want to tell you that there are state investigators here with recording devices. There's a man on the third row from the State Sovereignty Commission. There's another on the seventh row from the State Public Safety Department. They will take your picture. They will record your voice."

Suddenly he raised his voice an octave. "Don't worry! Talk! Tell Mr. Lowenstein everything! He wants to know the truth! Well, tell him! We don't have anything to hide!"

Dean sat to a roar of applause.

During the next two weeks, after the hearings started, I had to travel back and forth the one hundred some-odd miles between Tuscaloosa and Montgomery. By necessity, I missed much of the legal action. But every time I was present, Dean was magnificent. He defended his clients and students' rights generally with great clarity if not often with overblown dramatic emphasis, which delighted the students.

Ultimately, Dean showed through testimony from the witness stand that the Minnesota student whom I had earlier interviewed was indeed an undercover provacateur from the Federal Bureau of Investigation. The man had himself set fire to the ROTC building, an act, he said, designed to incite both students and the administration.

Because of this and other testimony, all but one of Dean's clients were exonerated. On appeal, the last one was also found innocent.

Through the years I came to have great respect for Dean's natural ability to recognize instantly an important news story.

It was that type of recognition that unfolded one afternoon as we rode eastward out of Montgomery toward Opelika and the Lee County Courthouse where Dean was to represent several Auburn University students in a drug case.

About two weeks earlier Dean had telephoned me from his wonderful live oak-shaded home on the banks of the Chocta-whatchee Bay. His good friend Chuck Morgan, who had a summer home only several hundred feet away, had been told by two Judge Advocate General staffers from the Pentagon that they had overheard conversations pertaining to a young lieutenant being held at Fort Benning in Georgia on charges of killing an entire village of South Vietnamese civilians. I convinced my editors at *The Alabama Journal* that this was "a big story," and they agreed to allow me one week to develop it. I drove some ninety miles southeast, discovered there was another reporter looking for the same story (that reporter turned out to be Seymore Hersh), and on my third day on Fort Benning I found 26-year-old pimply-faced First Lieutenant William Laws Calley. By the end of the week I had enough information to write: "A 26-year-old Army officer at Fort Benning, Ga., is being investigated on charges of 'the multiple murder of civilians in South Vietnam.'" The second graf stated that Calley was "suspected of wiping out an entire South Vietnamese village by killing 91 people — men, women, and children." This was the first big story in the Calley affair.

As I was riding with Dean, he began questioning me about what I had found and how I saw Calley, whom I had interviewed along with Hersh and *New York Times* reporter Jon Nordheimer. Within a few miles and several hundred words, Dean declared that he believed the Calley situation was the biggest legal happening in military history since Nazi leaders were tried and sentenced at Nuremburg after World War Two. We explored the moral questions. Already My Lai Four, where the men, women, and children were killed, was a household word. This story about a young man who had been put in charge of a platoon of soldiers with no more than an inkling of training involved a whole generation. For a decade boys-next-door had been hauled off to that God-forsaken country so far away nobody had heard of it before the first shot was fired. This story involved all of the young people: those who fought and lived, those who fought and died, and those who stayed home and fought the war by protesting in their own ways. Dean stated, "Calley is a catharsis of the Vietnam War. It's the biggest story of the decade." Before we knew it, Dean had driven past the Opelika exit on I-85 and we were in Georgia. We sped back to the Lee County Courthouse, where I called Calley's attorney, George Latimer, in Salt Lake City. He said he was sure his client would be interested in my doing a book with him.

In the next few months I signed a fifty-fifty contract with

Calley through a New York "book packager," interviewed Calley extensively in his apartment on Fort Benning and at my home in Montgomery, and wrote an outline and several sample chapters of our book. Ultimately, the fast-talker from the Big Apple gave me the old one-two right in the pocketbook. One Sunday morning I picked up a national supplement with the local newspaper and read in a gossip column where he had sold the Calley story to a book publisher, a magazine, and a movie production company at a high six-figure price. I called Dean, told him to take a look-see, and he advised me to write the agent immediately.

Several weeks later Dean, our old friend Chuck Morgan, and a New York attorney filed suit on my behalf. Some months later we settled out-of-court, I received a payment, and I obtained the rights to do my own book, which became *The Making of a Hero,* a sarcastic title which never caught hold of the public's imagination. Published by Touchstone in Louisville, Kentucky, the book was far from a runaway bestseller, although the sales were adequate. I was sent to sixteen cities across the country for television, radio, and newspaper interviews. My appearances and an aggressive sales representative made *Hero* a bestseller in Denver and the Rocky Mountain area, and it sold very well in the San Francisco Bay area and Los Angeles.

In the aftermath of *Hero's* success Touchstone also bought my second novel, *Hard Travelin',* about a campus troubadour during the 1960s, but the company folded its shop before the book was actually published.

Several years later, after recluse billionaire Howard Hughes died, Dean remembered that one of his major clients had been a distant kin to the man who built perhaps the largest financial empire in the free world.

Dean discovered that his client had been adopted when she was a small girl by her stepfather, Rupert Hughes, an uncle of Howard Hughes. This adoption, when the family lived in New York, was never legalized. However, the child and her brother both became Hughes, and she knew Howard as Cousin Buddy.

Armed with an agreement that he would share fifty-fifty in any portion of the Howard Hughes estate he would be able to get for his client, Dean sought to determine whether a New York adoption could be legal by common law. A young associate researched and found a nineteenth century law on the books, and through Dean's brilliance and determination made it stick.

For several years, operating on borrowed money and an iron-strong belief that he would win, Dean pursued the case. He found his client's brother in a California desert, living in a hovel and driving an ancient Buick with no windows. He signed representation papers with him for the same agreement as with his sister.

During these days and weeks and months Dean was a one-man show against a team of lawyers from Los Angeles to Houston to New York, all of whom were attempting constantly to shoot him down legally.

"After we finally proved our position, the time came to divide the percentages," he recalled. "We would determine exactly who would get what cut."

Dean prepared to meet with the top guns of Summa Corporation, Howard Hughes' umbrella company which had now been taken over by attorneys for heirs, led by Will Loomis, whose mother was Howard Hughes' first cousin and the closest of kin.

Before he left his Wilshire Boulevard hotel, Dean discovered he had forgotten a belt. He had on a fine suit, shirt, tie, shoes and socks, but no belt. "I felt naked without a belt," Dean remembered. "It's one of those things: you want to go into battle fully clothed."

He met another of the laywers in the lobby, told him he needed a belt, and they walked across the boulevard to a Rodeo Drive shop. When Dean asked the clerk for a belt, the man slipped a beautiful brown leather item from a rack. He held it up to Dean and said it went perfectly with his suit.

Dean slipped it through the loops and buckled it neatly. "How much?" he asked.

The clerk said it would be one hundred and twenty five dollars. Although Dean knew he had only one hundred and fifty on his person, he nodded. He pulled out the cash and handed it to the man.

At the meeting the attorneys began haggling over percentages. In some instances, they bickered back and forth over one-eighth and one-fourth percentages. Of course, this represented millions and millions of dollars down the road in possible moneys to be paid to various heirs.

Finally, when it came to Dean, he and Loomis became stuck somewhere between seven and ten percent. The negotiations went on and on into the afternoon.

When Dean stood, he commanded the floor. He was a tall, square-shouldered man with a big, dramatic face, custom-shagged gray hair, a tan suit and a gold-buckled belt, and a looseness about him that reminded the others of a championship basketball player. When he stepped in front of them, he was Larry Bird loping down the court, becoming airborne, and easily making a layup that would win the world title one more time. It didn't look difficult at all as he reached into his pocket and pulled out a half-dollar and flipped it into the air and allowed it to fall almost to the floor before he kicked it just at the right moment with the heel of his well-polished right shoe. It looked like he was born catching an end-over-end flashing half-dollar piece as he snatched it out of the air and slapped it down on top of his left hand.

"You call it," Dean said to Loomis. "Heads, my clients get twelve percent. Tails, they get seven percent."

Loomis, who was the spitting image of the legendary deal-maker Howard Hughes, minus the mustache, did not tremble. But he was shaken. "My God, George, we're talking about billions here."

Neither did Dean tremble. "Call it," he said, barely keeping his voice from breaking.

Within the next minute they settled on a percentage between the two extremes he had named. They shook hands.

From that moment on, Dean was a part of the Summa team.

Would he and his clients have gotten the larger or smaller percentage? He never knew. He put the coin into his pocket without checking how it lay.

In the aftermath, Dean and his lovely wife Jane settled in Chestertown, Maryland, on the Chesapeake Bay near where his brother David lived. At least once a month he flew to Houston and/or Las Vegas to examine the empire of which he became part owner. He and Jane renovated a magnificent old hotel on the main street of the tiny town, brought in the best French-style chef he could find on the east coast, and began re-doing a Federalist house to be a showplace. And in the midst of all the luxury he continued to see the big stories as they unfolded in the nearby capital, calling out constantly: "Somebody needs to find the behind-the-scenes real truth of the Contra affair . . ." or "I tell you, Oliver North knows more than he's telling . . ." or "Who will be the *real* candidate in the 1988 race for the presidency . . ." all long before the unfolding of the facts.

87

Lottie Lett

Note: The following article was published on the op-ed page of *The New York Times* on January 19, 1976.

She died. That's what they told me at the country store down the road from the empty house. Four years ago I was driving north on the strip of highway in rural Wilcox County in south Alabama when I saw smoke billowing up into the gray sky. As I passed I saw a black woman dipping clothes into a black pot under which a fire was smoldering. Within a hundred yards I stopped, turned around, and returned to her.

Her name was Lottie Lett. She was a great broad woman with a magnificent African face, stood about five feet six inches and had a bandanna tied about her hair. Her clothes were tattered but clean. She worked diligently with the pile of clothes on the scrubbed shelf near her wash pot. The smell of the burning hickory and scorched lye soap permeated the cool winter air.

"I was born way back yonder," she said, not remembering the exact day or year. "I was born right on this place. It belonged to the Simpsons then, the great-granddaddy of the people who live down in the big house now. My Mammy, she was a slave. I don't remember much about back then. It was a long time ago."

The best she could recall she was ninety years old, give or take two or three years. "Thank the Lord, I've always been in pretty good health. My old bones ache a little now and then, but I ain't ever been bed sick."

While she talked she wielded an old broomstick, stirring the clothes around and around in the smoke-capped pot. Now and then

89

she raised the stick and a white shirt or sheet clung to it, dropping slowly back into the liquid.

"This place is the same as it always was far as I can see," she said. The frame house behind her had never been painted, lacked underpinning and was without screens on the windows or doors. A makeshift stone chimney had been fashioned in a helter-skelter manner up the northern wall. Chickens danced about the yard that had no grass but was evenly lined where she had meticulously swept with a brush broom.

She had buried three men in her lifetime, she said, and had seven children scattered from Detroit to Newark to Birmingham. "They used to go off way up North. My first child went to Detroit when he was eighteen. He never did finish high school. Only thing for him around here was farming.

"Those ol' cotton rows get long out there. That's the kind of work that'll kill a fellow before he gets all his growing in. He went up to Detroit and went to work in a plant and came back down here driving a two-tone Buick. My oldest daughter went off to Atlanta, then went to Newark. She married a fellow that drives a truck up there. They've got a good bit of money, they come down here to see me, they've got seven young 'uns themselves. I've got twenty-two grandchildren all together."

Her face nearly glowed as she spoke the joyful words. She talked on and on about her various children, and finally said, "They used to go way off up North, but now the young 'uns go to the big cities of Birmingham and Mobile and they can come home more than the other ones."

A daughter died young and left her with a grandson to raise. He was fourteen, and he accounted for the large amount of white t-shirts and blue jeans that had to be washed. "I just keep on working," she said with determined resignation. "If I didn't have something to do every day when I get up I'd shrivel up and get blown away by the wind." She smiled as she said the words.

"When I was a little girl, times were tougher than they are now," she said later in front of the fireplace in the simply furnished living room. She had poured homemade scuppernong wine into peanut butter glasses. We drank the sweet liquid and she talked.

"My Mammy was a slave, she worked in the house, tended to the children, cooked food for the Simpsons, and I did the same thing.

"When I was little, I'd go there with Mammy and I'd play with the white children. When we got up seven or eight years old they went off to their school. I went to school for two years. Nobody cared whether colored children went to school or not in Wilcox County back then. I just didn't go to school anymore. I stayed home and took care of my brothers and sisters while Mammy worked at the big house.

"I don't remember my Daddy. Mammy said he was a slave too. He left when I was a little girl. He went up North, best I recollect. Seemed like everybody went up North if they got a chance.

"I've been to Montgomery. I never went to Birmingham. I never went to Mobile. I go in to Camden ever so often.

"I never did want to leave down here. This is my home. I've lived here all my years. I churn my butter out on that porch. I wash those clothes out in the yard. I like to hear the whippoorwills calling and the mockingbirds answering. I milk that ol' cow over yonder, and she gives a fair amount of milk. When they kill a hog down at the big house they send me some fatback and part of a ham. I usually ask if I can clean up some chitlins. I like good, clean, fried chitlins. In the winter I make some collards in the patch, and they sure are good with chitlins," she said.

She was proud of the picture of Dr. Martin Luther King Jr. her daughter had given to her. She displayed it over the mantel, and she said he was the greatest black man who ever lived.

When I drove to the house this winter it was empty. I walked across the yard. I sat on the steps and looked across the road to the pasture beyond. I remembered her words.

Tobacco-Chewing Judge

Note: This profile appeared on the Viewpoint page of *The Baltimore Sun* in 1978.

Not long after U.S. District Judge Frank M. Johnson Jr. of Alabama was picked by President Carter to succeed Clarence M. Kelley as director of the FBI, the judge's brother Jimmy asked if he would be taking his two Great Danes to Washington with him. The judge answered simply, "Yep, I sure am."

When Jimmy persisted, asking, "Are you going to chew tobacco in Washington like you do down here?" the six-foot-one-inch tall judge replied, "Yes, I am."

This is part of Mr. Johnson's personality which he holds dear. He is a quiet individualist. He is a learned and complex man. He is strong in his deep-seated self-control. Nearly three years ago, after smoking three packs of Home Run cigarettes daily, he threw half a pack of the harsh-tasting tobacco out the window of his car and swore off. He has not touched a cigarette since. He has taken up the chewing of plug tobacco.

His friend, former American Civil Liberties Union attorney Charles Morgan Jr., who now practices in Washington, calls Mr. Johnson a man who came out of the "free state of Winston County," which tried to secede from Alabama when the state seceded from the Union, and who had the courage to bring lawfulness to a countryside that wanted nothing to do with the federal law. "It took somebody who didn't have to pay the social tax most other Southerners of the middle fifties and sixties thought they had to pay," Mr. Morgan said.

Mr. Johnson came out of the hill country of north Alabama,

93

where his grandfather, James Wallace "Straight Edge" Johnson, had been sheriff and his father, Frank Sr., had been probate judge. His father was later elected to the state House of Representatives where he served a full term as the only Republican among more than one hundred members.

After wrecking two cars when he was a teenager, Mr. Johnson was sent to Gulf States Military Academy in Gulfport, Mississippi, and after graduation worked as a surveyor and attended Massey Business College in Birmingham.

Mr. Johnson was nineteen years old when he married a pretty farm girl from his home county, Ruth Jenkins, and they worked their way through the University of Alabama undergraduate school. One of their friends was George C. Wallace, who was to become the most powerful governor in the state's history and who was to shake his fist at Mr. Johnson's federal court.

During law school days Mr. Johnson and Mr. Wallace became close friends. With the third member of their triumvirate, Glen Curlee, who was to be appointed judge and later district attorney of Elmore County by Wallace, they enjoyed talking politics until the wee hours.

At an Alabama-Tennessee football game, Curlee was arrested by a policeman for being drunk. At night court, Johnson acted as Curlee's counsel and Wallace was star witness. After Wallace testified that Curlee had had nothing to drink, the policeman took the stand. As Wallace recalls in his autobiography, *Stand Up For America,* Johnson was even then a superb lawyer. Cross-examining, Johnson asked, "Isn't it a fact, officer, that you saw very few students or other persons drunk at the ball game?"

The policeman said, "Of course I saw drunks. There were drunks everywhere. Hundreds of them. You had to be blind not to see them."

"Is there an ordinance in Birmingham that requires you to arrest a man who is publicly drunk?" asked Johnson.

"Of course there is. That's why I arrested this man," the officer stated.

"How many other arrests did you make that day, other than Mr. Curlee?"

"One."

"What for?"

"For public drunkenness."

94

"You mean the law in Birmingham says you must arrest a public drunk, and you saw several hundred drunks while you were on patrol duty, and you arrested only two — and one of them was really sober?"

The judge found Curlee innocent of the charges. Afterward, the judge invited the students to his home. While Wallace and Johnson enjoyed a drink, Curlee, who liked a shot of whiskey or bottle of beer as well as most men, was offered only coffee or Coke. The defense, he complained later, had been too good.

That was during the days when the men were friends. Later, after Johnson became federal judge in Montgomery, following a stint in the Army and in law practice and as assistant U.S. attorney in Birmingham, he and Wallace became foes.

When the U.S. Civil Rights Commission asked for the voting records of the counties where Wallace was circuit judge, Wallace refused to hand them over. Johnson ordered Wallace to turn over the records or show cause why he shouldn't be held in contempt.

With Curlee as go-between, Wallace arranged to meet Johnson at the Johnson home. Wallace offered to stand fast "if you'll give me a light sentence." Johnson, unblinking, told him, "If you don't hand over those records, I'll throw the book at you, George."

Early the next morning, Wallace called his grand juries together. He gave them the records. He then went before Johnson, who found that Wallace was not in contempt because he had produced the records "by devious means." He stated that "this court refuses to allow its authority and dignity to be bent or swayed by such politically generated whirlwinds."

Outside the courthouse, Wallace told reporters that Johnson was an "integrating, carpetbagging, scalawagging, race-mixing, bold-faced liar." Not many years later, after Wallace became governor and after Johnson had found in favor of the Reverend Martin Luther King Jr. in the Montgomery bus boycott and other cases, the two men had other confrontations.

In a massive opinion, Johnson allowed the Selma-to-Montgomery march to take place. "The law is clear that the right to petition one's government for redress of grievances may be exercised in large groups," he wrote. Wallace angrily lambasted the judge again, but the march took place.

Johnson's orders desegregated schools in Alabama, reapportioned the Legislature, and called for equal hiring practices by the state police in the Department of Public Safety. Johnson sat on the three-judge panel that struck down Alabama's poll-tax law, which unfairly burdened poor people by not allowing them to vote unless they had money to pay for the right.

After suits were brought in the Middle District of Alabama, Johnson took over the administration of both the state mental health and prison departments. These decisions led editorialists to call him "the real governor of Alabama." He not only ruled that the departments were constitutionally inadequate and unhealthy, he set down stringent guidelines he expected them to follow. Since then, he has in effect been the administrator of the departments, which even later became models after which other states molded their mental institutions and prisons.

Again, Wallace sounded his disapproval. After the prison opinion, Wallace said that the federal courts were trying to turn prisons into country clubs. He suggested that "some federal judges need a barbed-wire enema."

According to Chuck Morgan, who had little criticism of Judge Johnson, "He will bring to the FBI what he gave to the Middle District of Alabama. In the sense of the United States, he was an outpost here. Frank Johnson believes in the equal protection amendment of the Constitution, and as director he will provide equal protection for all."

And as Alabama civil rights attorney George W. Dean Jr. said when he heard that Johnson had been named to the FBI post, "God pity the Mafia."

Note: I contracted with Prentice-Hall to write a biography of Johnson. It was titled *The New G-Man: Frank M. Johnson Jr. of the FBI*. Just as I finished the final chapter, Judge Johnson called me and said he was withdrawing his name. He had been plagued with poor health for several months and did not think he had the strength to give the job all the energy he thought it deserved. Later he was appointed to the U.S. Circuit Court where he continued to make a name for himself as a thoughtful jurist.

Capote Country

Author's Note: In the late 1960s I wrote *Capote Country* for *Southern Voices* magazine, which was published in Atlanta by Southern Regional Council. Here it is with slight revision.

When he talked about his Alabama hometown, Truman Capote spoke in precious, porcelain words. "All of those people did the craziest, wildest things, and they called it ordinary," he said, smiling coyly as he spoke. "In their own way they're the quaintest population in the entire world. I love them. I really do."

His voice was reminiscent of the high-pitched drawl of south-west Alabama. "My aunts and cousins, the people that I knew there, all adore each other. I think they're very fond of me. I don't think there's a jealous bone in their bodies."

Riding into Monroeville, past the serene oak-shaded cemetery, the First Methodist Church, and the ancient red-brick courthouse, I felt an acute case of deja vu. Only the week before I had reread the short stories of *A Tree of Night* and *Breakfast at Tiffany's*, and with each turn of the head I saw a glimpse of some perfect paragraph.

In the sixties it was still a one-horse town. Far from a metropolis. A crossroads stop on Alabama rural routes, it was basically the same town it was more than a quarter of a century earlier. At that time it was not the boom town that people see today.

Billy Langsley was a local shopkeeper who went to elementary school and played during summer vacations with Capote when they were children. Capote's maternal kinfolks who still lived in Monroeville "are some of the nicest and some of the most wayout people you'd ever want to meet in your life.

"I haven't seen him (Capote) in, Lord, I don't know when. He comes around. Visits Nell (Harper) Lee (Pulitzer Prize-winning author of *To Kill A Mockingbird*), and we hear about it through the Monroe *Journal*. They had a picture of him a couple of years ago with Nell and his Jaguar. Boy, he was something else," said Langsley.

"When we were young it wasn't much different from any other kids growing up in a little town in the South. At least, I didn't think it was. I've read some of Truman's stories, and I don't think it was much like that around here. We used to go over to the Faulk's house — his mother was a Faulk, and he lived with some aunts and an uncle. We'd get milk and tea cakes and sit on the back steps and talk about crazy stories Truman's Great-Uncle Jim Henderson used to tell us. He was Truman's mother's uncle, and he was about the best storyteller in this part of the country. I'll guarantee you, I'll introduce you to some folks who've sat and listened to a-many of Jim Henderson's stories. And I guarantee you, Truman's heard plenty of them."

Jim was a drinking man, the people of the community related. As far as most folks knew, he was too good — especially when he was into the bottle, which apparently was most of the time. He was a hard-living human being and a fast talker. The story went that Uncle Jim traded the last portion of the family plantation for a keg of whiskey. A few years later, it was told, Uncle Jim died while sleeping on the back porch of a relative's house, his head resting on a roll of chicken wire.

Truman Copote's first cousin, John Byron Carter, a short, muscular, handsome policeman in Monroeville, told about Uncle Jim while we sat in canebottom chairs on the front porch of his old farmhouse on the outskirts of town.

John Byron, stoic and iron-jawed on first meeting, was not exactly eager to talk. He had had reporters sneaking around his town and homestead before. He had dealt with them through a silent veneer. But down-home acting can take a two-way street, and before we knew it we were calling each other "good ol' boy" and patting each other on the back.

Standing in his sleeveless t-shirt in the simple but comfortable kitchen, with a nameless four-month-old raccoon scampering around his feet on the bare hardwood floor, he poured two straight shots of fine Kentucky bourbon which we knocked back with the first cup of black coffee. He was preparing to go to church, he said, explaining with a grin, "I sing in the choir and this opens up my throat."

As we sat at the big mahogany dining room table, the raccoon tiptoed away to play with John Byron's children. John Byron hunched forward, stretching his back and arms and thick neck, and looked into his coffee as though it were a crystal ball. "I've read everything Truman has written," he said. "I guess you could say he got about more than half of what he has written from Monroeville and the family." He grinned again. "Of course, you won't get too many folks to admit that, but I believe it's true." Over his shoulder an antique bookcase came into focus. I recognized many of the original hardcover Capote spines.

"You take that story, 'A Grass Harp.' Something like that was always happening with our great aunts, especially Nannie Rumbley Faulk, whom Truman called Miss Sook in the story, 'A Christmas Memory.' In my opinion, Truman exaggerated a little — but not really very much. He's a reporter more than a fiction writer. Always has been. *The Muses Are Heard* and *In Cold Blood* aren't his only non-fiction by a long shot."

Finished with whiskey and coffee, he pushed the chair away from the table. He excused himself and invited me back for Sunday lunch, which everybody in that neck of the woods called "Sunday dinner," a ritual I remembered with fondness from my own childhood in north Alabama. I eagerly accepted.

In the meantime, John Byron pointed me in the right direction to retrace a backwoods dirt road which had been familiar to the youthful Capote. It was a road of yesterday. In time past, buggies, flatbed wagons, horseless carriages all had made their way in and out of these willow-lined curves. Even in midmorning sunlight I became chilled with thought, hearing the echoes of an experience Truman Capote might have known.

It was a sweet sound, a lilting voice of a spring wind sweeping across a flat meadow filled with sage grass and spotted with black-eyed susans. It was a sad song, a hummingbird's buzz in the honeysuckle vines on a lazy hot summer afternoon when little children lay in the shade of umbrella-shaped trees. It was a remembering, a tale of old folks dying in winter's last days, just before the frost went away and sunshine filtered over that low-lying knoll where a Negro boy was hung just before the turn of the century.

This was a beautiful, remarkable, complex country. It was a perfect country for the likes of Truman Streckfus Persons Capote. Such names as Murder Creek, Burnt Corn community, Fort Mims massacre, Chief Red Eagle of the Creeks peppered conversations. The land was scarred with human tragedy. Back in July of 1813 a group of white soldiers attacked a party of Indians who were returning from a trading venture in Pensacola. The attack took place on Burnt Corn Creek, and thirty-three days later the Indians took revenge with an attack on Fort Mims in Baldwin County. Before the end of the day, the Creeks had slaughtered about five hundred and fifty men, women, and children, and sent a shock wave through the southwestern frontier. The gossip of Monroeville told about a little girl who was kidnapped and brutally murdered and thrown into a creek to the north. The father of the girl, so the legend went, found the murderer before the law enforcement authorities and killed him and dumped him into the same creek. Thus the name, Murder Creek. The stories continued.

It was no wonder Capote found the place fascinating.

The backwoods road on which I traveled had been used years ago by Capote and his mother, whom he described as "very, very beautiful — a beauty-contest-winner type of child who later on in life became an enormously sensitive person. She was only sixteen when she was married — a normal, beautiful girl, rather wild — and my father was twenty-four." Born January 29, 1905, in Monroeville, her maiden name was Lillie Mae Faulk, and she was raised by three old maid aunts and a bachelor uncle in a house on the big curve on the road to Mobile.

Although he adopted his stepfather's name, Capote, it was made apparent by visiting the town and talking to the people who knew him that he identified strongly with his father. His young mother met and married J. Archie Persons while both were students at Troy Normal School, now Troy State University. A pale, short, heavy-set, almost bald man in his late sixties when I met him, he lived in Baton Rouge, Louisiana. While talking he periodically pursed sun-speckled lips, not unlike a personality trait of his son. And he loved to talk. In both looks and personality, one could easily see an older image of the famous son.

100

Second cousin to former Governor Gordon Persons, Arch said, "I am known far and wide throughout the South as a super salesman." In a high-pitched sing-song voice, he told of being a steamboat captain on the Mississippi River when Truman was born in New Orleans on September 30, 1924. "He was a beautiful little fellow. His mother had him dressed up in a sailor suit with a white straw hat. Truman was a dandy, and he could do a tap dance about as soon as he could walk. He was a little bitty fellow. Even then he knew how to put on a show. He loved to have an audience. We named him for the steamship company I worked for — Streckfus." Of that, Archie remained very proud, although, he said, he did not understand why Truman took such a "Mafia name" as Capote when he could have remained an "Alabama Persons."

"From the time he was a baby I knew he'd be successful. He had it in him. When you're born with it, you have it forever," said Arch Persons. "I've been a go-getter all my life. I've been into a little bit of everything. I've made some good money, and I've lost some, but I always was trying — just like Truman. I bet before (he's finished) he'll sell more books than anybody else who writes 'em."

After his mother and father divorced, Truman was brought to Monroeville. He was about five years old, and as his aunt, John Byron Carter's mother, Mrs. Mary Ida Carter, said, "He was discovering the world. He was into everything any normal boy would be into — and then some."

When John Byron Carter had her for Sunday dinner that day, she laughed lightly and said, "Truman's told us just to agree with anything anybody asks us — especially a reporter." Then she laughed again. During dinner, when she saw that I had a third helping of fried chicken without a usual outsider's embarrassment and spinned a little yarn about how I used to eat fresh loin after hog-killing at my Granddaddy's, she opened up.

"Oh, you ought to have seen him when he first came home with Lillie Mae. He was all dressed up fit-to-kill. Looked like some kind of doll you can buy at the five-and-dime. Looked kind of funny, to tell the truth, but he was smart as a whip. You could tell that immediately.

"He was always telling the biggest tales. Even when he was six, seven years old. He's come home and tell about something happening. It'd scare the living fool out of all of us, but nine times out of ten it'd turn out to be just something he'd made up in his

101

head. Later on, I reckon, it was that kind of thing that made him so great."

John Byron entered the story. "I was younger than Truman, and I used to tag along behind him and the older boys. But he looked as young as me. And he was always sort of sensitive. When we'd go fishing we'd give Truman the worms to bait the hooks. Sometimes we'd squash the worms just to watch him make a face and draw back."

On this Sunday afternoon I found the Burnt Corn community like a ghost village. Once the center of a rich farming area, on this day the beautifully elegant little frame church was empty, several houses appeared abandoned, one rambling house with a wide porch sat amid a thicket of trees, and a freshly painted white Baptist Church, built in 1821, was known as the new church. There was a gothic darkness about the place, a yesterday antique feeling. There was a strangeness about a simple sycamore tree standing in the front yard of an empty house. When he was a boy Capote visited here at least once. Another aunt in Monroeville, Mrs. Lucille Ingram, showed me the clipping from the society pages of the Monroe County *Journal*. The story told of a birthday party for an elderly lady in Burnt Corn. The last paragraph read, "As a fitting highlight of the occasion, little Truman Persons scampered in with an armload of presents . . ."

Standing next to the old church and cemetery, it was not difficult to imagine the first seeds of Capote's most lyrical and descriptive stories being planted during visits here. I thought of the bus rounding Deadman's Curve in "Children on their Birthdays," but an hour later the aunt, Mrs. Ingram, said the curve was one which existed in front of the old Faulk Place, which had since been razed for a new asphalt shopping center parking lot.

Capote finished the first grade at Monroeville Elementary School, and afterwards was sent to a military school in Greenwich, Connecticut. In the lonely isolation of the private school he began writing about the nostalgia of leaving his beloved friend, Miss Nannie Rumbley Faulk, also known as Miss Sook. Years later his powerful, heart-tugging reminiscenes, "A Christmas Memory" and "The Thanksgiving Visitor," were successfully translated to film by director Frank Perry. Both stories were filmed in Alabama near Montgomery, and I tell about that in another part of this book.

Capote spent summers with Miss Sook and two other aunts, Miss Caroline Elizabeth Faulk and Virginia Hurd Faulk, and an uncle, Richard Howard Faulk, his mother's closest relatives. During one summer, Mrs. Ingram recalled, a little girl who lived down the street got hit by a bus on the curve no more than a hundred yards from the Faulk house.

The writer once told of a time "I ran away with a friend who lived across the street — a girl much older than myself who in later years achieved a certain fame — because she murdered a half-dozen people and was electrocuted at Sing Sing. Someone wrote a book about her. They called her the Lonelyhearts Killer. I can't recall her name, but I was fascinated with her. She cared for me also, like most people who are in trouble care for each other."

His Aunt Mary Ida, John Byron's mother, who rode around the country roads on a big and powerful Triumph motorcycle, remembered, "I don't know how old he was. Must have been twelve or thirteen. He and that girl went off to . . . let me see where . . ." She thought it was "some exotic place like Atmore or Frisco City," both small towns south of Monroeville. "He and that girl — she later turned out to be a gun moll or something — they stayed at a hotel down there."

When I asked Harper Lee, Capote's closest friend, about the runaway escapade, she said, "I don't remember his running away with any girl." She frowned slightly, then a grin came to her face. "He must have been about eight. We were having a fuss. He ran away with another little girl. They hitchhiked to Evergreen (about twenty miles to the east, past Burnt Corn), but they were back by supper."

Miss Velma Dees, a pleasant, spectacled, retired school-teacher, tutored him one summer. Capote was having trouble with mathematics and Miss Dees said that she had fun "attempting to teach him while his mind was a thousand miles away."

When he was ten or twelve years old he sold his first story, a roman a clef about the life in Monroeville, to the Mobile *Press-Register.* Entitled "Old Mr. Busybody," it won a five-dollar prize and "caused somewhat of a scandal around town," according to Aunt Mary Ida.

Harper Lee, whose novel, *To Kill A Mockingbird,* was also about a thinly disguised Monroeville with a fascinating character much like the youthful Capote, remembered, "When we were a bit too young to read, Brother, who was a voracious reader, would read many, many stories to us. Then we'd dramatize the stories in our own ways, and Truman would always provide the necessary comic relief to break up the melodrama. Actually, we were the only children on the street of an adult neighborhood. For a while there was the girl across the street, but she didn't live there long. Of course, being the outsiders made it interesting for us. We were able to watch people better. That was our main interest: people watching."

Miss Lee, who assisted Capote in his tedious research for *In Cold Blood* about the violent murders of an entire family in rural Kansas and about the killers who were tracked down and later executed, traced the Indian history of Monroe County and told about half-breeds who used to live on the other side of the town. She said she and Truman Capote visited places with Miss Sook and the people and the places impressed them both. "Truman has — and always will have — an enormous amount of curiosity. Anything unusual interests him," she said.

Miss Dees, his tutor, said Capote could draw pictures like no other student she had ever had. "He was all-around talented. I recognized that immediately. His drawings were wonderful. They showed that imagination that has come out so nicely in his stories."

His imagination blossomed early with the tales that alarmed the household. "Once he came in in a frenzy. In a breathless way, he told us about a mad gypsy who had run into the courthouse square screaming in an unknown tongue," his Aunt Mary Ida said. "Of course, there was no gypsy. It was just another one of his stories, but he had us all hopping around there for a while. He liked to stir us up — for one reason or another."

Author's Note: In 1965 and again in 1967 I had the privilege of meeting Capote, talking with him, and also meeting and knowing movie director Frank Perry. In May of 1968, *Status* magazine in New York published my article entitled "TV Quartet by Truman Capote."

For more than a half-hour the weary, mud-caked technical crew worked to clear debris from the innards of the old house which was being used as a set for Truman Capote's "The Thanksgiving Visitor."

104

Finally they had the unnecessary antiques piled in an out-of-the-way corner, the lights set correctly and props in place in the makeshift kitchen that looked like it had just stepped out of the 1930s.

The director, a short, rather chunky man with his raven hair falling over his eyes, his mustache uneven over his upper lip, and his bare stomach poking out naked between his low-slung stained polo shirt, climbed to a crouched position next to the huge camera. He teetered there in his position as he looked on the scene and his youthful actor-star whose blonde hair fell in bangs over his forehead like an exact miniature replica of the play's author. The director, still swaying back and forth, reached out toward the actor with his left hand. His fingers groped at the air. His expression became exaggeratedly painful.

"You have just been hurt, Buddy. Terribly hurt!" he said, almost squeaking with remorse, almost crying with pity for the predicament of the character.

"Lean forward slightly," he directed.

His small, dark eyes, visibly tired with slack and shadows beneath them, went down to the camera. He sighted his subject through the lens. "Now, Buddy, move," he said gently.

And the boy moved ever so slowly, tediously drawing himself close to tears.

"Perfect," the director whispered.

He moved back to his teetering position and let the cameraman have his place. "Now, again!" he said.

"Quiet!" shouted the assistant director.

"Let's shoot," the director said. "Camera! Action!"

The camera rolled.

The boy moved, slowly, slowly, his eyes watering.

Only two minutes, and the director shouted, "Cut! Print it!"

He came down from his standing place. After a quick hug for his actor-star, he turned to me. The weariness faded suddenly into a smile. "It's a wrap," Frank Perry said, laying that same expressive left hand on my shoulder.

He looked directly into my eyes, and the smile seemed to grow across his face. "We're through," he said again, as though he could hardly believe it himself.

This man who had spent most of the past two years putting four short stories by Truman Capote on film was at the end of another short but meaningful chapter of his thirty-seven-year-old life.

"This one is going to be the best. It's beautiful. You should see it, Wayne," he said. His words were staccato and yet soft against the undercurrent of the quick shuffling of the technical men, blue-jeaned and dirty, tired but still working hard to clean away the last of the equipment.

"This one has Truman's special kind of humor in it," Perry said. "It's different from the others. It's beautiful. It really is."

His enthusiasm over the project of the television film, "The Thanksgiving Visitor," did not let up. It poured out as we walked across the muddy back lawn of the old house in the southern part of Montgomery County in central Alabama.

Standing next to his rented station wagon, Frank Perry peered toward the big house in the darkness. In the light of the full moon we had a marvelously sentimental silhouette of the two-storied one-hundred-year-old farmhouse.

"The house is the star of the show," Frank said. The same enthusiasm continued to bubble from him. It is his trademark, his way of life. And it is why, I imagined at that moment, all of these people — from Capote to the obscure light man — enjoyed working with him.

About three months earlier the producer, director, and principal owner of Francis Productions Inc. in New York had telephoned me on a drizzly slow Sunday morning and asked if I would help find locations for another Capote film.

I nearly leapt out of my skin and through the long distance wire, I couldn't wait to get on the highway in search of what he described as an "high-ceilinged, Victorian, shabby but imposing old farmhouse, but *not* with a plantation feeling or an antebellum look. It should be in a lovely, bucolic, agrarian setting, and, if possible, should be empty, since we will be shooting at this one location for seventy-five percent of the picture — at least ten days."

I started looking that afternoon, searching out little-used roads in the southern part of the county.

While I looked I kept in mind that I was doing a menial but important task for a man who was a perfectionist. I had worked with Frank Perry before when he was in the area shooting "A Christmas Memory," which had become television legend. With this single one-hour show he had proved his genius for bringing to

106

the visual surface the precious heart-tugging feelings which Capote evoked in his writings. Critics in big cities and one-horse villages alike had praised the Christmas drama. And it had been slated by ABC as an annual event for ten years.

Besides this picture he had put two more Capote pieces on film, "Among the Paths to Eden," and "Miriam."

Riding and thinking about the man, I felt that it would be impossible to find the right house for the story, which I read the next day. Frank Perry was depending on me to come up with something worthwhile, and I continued to feel horribly inadequate. After almost two weeks of house-hunting, and even after Perry's assistant, Lynn Foreman, came South to help look, I was almost ready to give up. Cursing myself and the quick-falling sun on the day I had proclaimed to be the last, I made the swift decision at an intersection to turn south instead of heading for home. Sitting out there on a little knoll was the most beautiful old ramshackled palace I had ever seen; and it appeared empty. I slammed on my brakes, jumped out and snapped photos from every angle.

I mailed these pictures and within several days Frank came to Montgomery and we tramped across the rain-soaked front yard (by now, with the owner's permission). The house was falling down and covered with manure, as it had been the home to about a dozen goats in the pasture. But Frank seemed not to see the goats and cared not one bit about the manure. His face was excited. "It looks just perfect," he said. "It has character. Those lines . . ."

"Look at those walls," Frank said. "Why Gene Callahan (the set decorator who had won Academy Awards for his work on "The Hustler" and "America, America") will be able to do wonders with these old rooms."

Two weeks from that day he was back in Alabama with a crew of about forty technicians and a half-dozen actors, including Geraldine Page who had starred as Miss Sook in "A Christmas Memory," a role which she would portray again in this story. By now the tall, bearded, immaculate Callahan had the house turned into a dream from the memory of Truman Capote.

Several days later, when Capote arrived on the set with his traveling companion, Princess Lee Radziwill, he went into the Callahan-decorated kitchen with Perry and exclaimed, "I sat at that very table. This *is* my old home place. It is! I lived in a place just like this when I was growing up."

107

And Frank Perry beamed. He turned to me and winked. We had an understanding as far as this house was concerned, and minutes later he introduced me to Capote and said I was playing the newly created role of Cousin Wayne. Capote tapped my arm and said, "Oh, I had a cousin just like you."

That afternoon the shooting of the movie continued. Capote sat dressed in a lemon-colored turtleneck, orange trousers, and brown multi-zippered carcoat and observed the work.

In his high-pitched, nasal sing-song, Capote said, "Frank Perry is the only movie man who understands my stories. He does them magnificently. He knows the meaning of every tiny detail, and with him the screen versions become true collaborations.

"Did you see 'A Christmas Memory'?" he asked.

I nodded.

"Well, you could see that he knew what he was doing. He chose the perfect setting. And he had the right actors. In it Geraldine *is* Miss Sook, just as she is in this story. And the boy, Michael Kearney there (he pointed toward the young actor-star of 'Thanksgiving') is me when I was a boy. He looks exactly like me." (Michael, who also starred as the lad in "All the Way Home," was romping across the front lawn with his spotted dog from the film.)

"And when Frank gets all the characters down on the film he knows exactly how to edit. He knows when and where to chop. In fact, he's so good that it comes out like a picture poem.

"When I saw 'A Christmas Memory' I cried. I really did. It was such an excellent job. I had never been more pleased with anything of mine done for the screen." (He had written "Beat The Devil" especially for the movies and it had starred Humphrey Bogart under the direction of John Huston.)

"With that effort I thought Frank had squeezed every moment into the span of fifty-six minutes, which is the actual length that it ran. He got in all the pathos, all the tender feeling and all the rapture of that almost forgotten moment of nostalgia which is childhood.

"I had seen his work, his first movie 'David and Lisa,' which I thought was one of the most profound movies made in this country. And I had heard him talk. He talks well. And I was sure he could translate my work to the screen. Of course, he did."

Capote spoke of his co-screenwriter and Frank's wife, Eleanor

Perry. Together Capote and Mrs. Perry had won an Emmy for best teleplay for their adaptation of "A Christmas Memory."

"She is a lovely writer," Capote said. "She respects my wishes in the plays. And she too understands my work. She ponders over the details on paper just as Frank sweats out the artistic decisions on film.

"She did the screenplay for 'David and Lisa,' which was a really superb job. And with us together, how could we miss?"

Capote grinned broadly. It was a friendly and Southern grin. It was a proud grin.

The next day Frank and Eleanor Perry surprised the author with a family reunion picnic in the pastureland setting. Twenty of Capote's relatives from all over Alabama had arrived. The author greeted them and seated them on a massive tiger-striped rug. But they had to wait to eat. The last guest had not arrived.

After a moment, on the horizon of a golden Alabama hill, Princess Lee Radziwill appeared astride a sorrel mare. With her was the owner of the property, Dr. Woody Bartlett, a local veterinarian, and they cantered to the picnic, where Capote and the Perrys met them.

The director, although he obviously enjoyed the fun, was eager to get back to his position next to the camera. The mustachioed director who began his career on a drama scholarship at the University of Miami (where he taught classes even as an undergraduate) excused himself and strode toward the house and work, the fast pace of his step another indication of the man who pushes himself all the way at every minute.

During his senior year at Miami he dropped out of school to open a winter stock theater in the Bahamas. As he recalled, it was a success as that type of thing goes; but he could not stick with it long enough to really make it pay.

The Korean Conflict broke out and he went with it. He was no more than an average soldier, he said; he got his meager check, had his fun, joined in the fights, and before he knew it was discharged.

Soon after he came home, he took a job parking cars at a country playhouse in Pennsylvania. He had to stay close to theater, and he soon met most of those working with the company. He so impressed them that in 1954, at the age of twenty-three, he became an apprentice stage manager at the playhouse.

With Joseph Anthony, the successful director, Perry arrived on Broadway as assistant stage manager of "The Rainmaker," which starred Geraldine Page.

It was Miss Page who later recommended him to the Actors Studio where he associated with actors and actresses of the calibre of Marlon Brando, James Dean, Marilyn Monroe, and Rod Steiger. Here he developed his acting and consequently his directing talents.

This student episode of his life ended when he went to work with the Theatre Guild as stage manager. In that capacity he worked with "Requiem for a Nun," "Sunrise at Campobello," "Bells Are Ringing," and "The Third Best Sport."

The last play was written by the slight, delicate lady with the soft and intelligent voice who later would become his wife. And when they were married they became a team which would conquer the movie-making establishment.

About two years after they were married, after selling a movie idea to Hollywood, the couple paid a down payment of $500 as an option on the screen rights to a short psychological case study entitled *Lisa and David.*

"While Eleanor wrote the screenplay during the summer — we were both very confident then — I begged and borrowed the money to make the movie as an independent production.

"The film, which we called 'David and Lisa,' was made in twenty-five days of shooting. And at the end of that I felt it was a disaster."

Still, he took the finished product to the Venice Film Festival, "where we turned it on its ears." He came away with the laurels of Best New Director, and the show won numerous other awards.

But the Perrys, who thrived on work (Eleanor: "He loves to spend hour after hour, day after day, week after week, editing the films that he has made." Frank: "She's the most professional writer for the screen in this land."), could not rest with their success.

They formed Francis Productions Inc. and they set out to make another feature-length movie, "Lady Bug . . . Lady Bug," about children with the threat of the bomb hanging over their heads.

"Actually I think it is better than 'David and Lisa,'" Frank said. "But I'm afraid it was a financial flop."

But even that did not stop him. It seemed to have only aged him, matured him and ended another chapter. It enabled him to take a firm grip on his situation and latch onto the Capote properties.

"I had read Truman's stories when I was going to school, and I thought they were real gems. They were true, genuine and so damned poetic . . . especially 'A Christmas Memory,' which continued to haunt me.

"Later, after I did get to meet Truman, I mentioned the possibility of filming the stories. But something happened. We were busy on something else, or he was busy. I don't remember exactly.

"But fate meant for us to be drawn together, and we later clicked with what we wanted. We came up with the same ideas, and Truman, Eleanor and I became partners."

The first three one-hour television specials produced by that partnership were "Memory," "Miriam," and "Among the Paths to Eden," which were re-edited and put into the framework of a movie-length feature under the title "Truman Capote's Trilogy."

As Frank Perry worked on "Visitor," Geraldine Page sat on the back steps of the big house and watched him. She smiled endearingly and said, "When I work with Frank, it's like I'm on vacation. And when it's all over, I know I've done my best work."

Author's Note: Since this story was written, Frank Perry made a number of movies. Among them were "The Swimmer" with Burt Lancaster, "Last Summer," "Mommie Dearest," and "Play It As It Lays."

Frank and Eleanor Perry were divorced after he made "Doc" with Stacy Keach from a screenplay by Pete Hamill. Eleanor wrote a bitter novel called *Blue Pages* in which she described a terrible marriage between a female writer of screenplays and a movie director. Later she died in New York after a long and painful battle with cancer. Frank married journalist Barbara Goldsmith, who wrote *Poor Little Rich Girl* and *Johnson Vs. Johnson,* and he continued to make fine movies.

Truman Capote visited Alabama several more times, the last when he was ill and had to be hospitalized in Montgomery. He died at the home of his friend, Joanna Carson, Johnny Carson's ex-wife, in California in 1985.

A Lady Friend

She's quite a lady.

She lies there quietly on the blue and gold print couch and barely moves. She rolls her eyes lazily and stares out the big windows at the pecan trees outside and the squirrels she has grown accustomed to over the years.

Her name is Zelda Sayre Fitzgerald Greenhaw and she's twenty-one years old. Not *that* old, one might think. But ancient for a chocolate-point Siamese feline who has done a fair amount of traveling in her day.

I was never a cat person. I liked dogs. When I was a boy I heard about my daddy putting kerosene on the tail of one of my aunt's cats and making it run for the nearest tree, and I laughed until my side hurt. Another time Daddy told about tying a can to a cat's tail and watching it fight in agony for release, and again I laughed. Such tales would not have been funny if told about a dog. The cat was the brunt of our country jokes.

However, when I was married at age twenty-five my young wife wanted a kitten. I came home one afternoon with this little ball of white fur. She was tiny with only a speck of dark tuft here and there. I announced that she had been born several doors from the house where F. Scott and Zelda Fitzgerald lived on Felder Avenue here in Montgomery, and my wife said, "Her name's Zelda," and thus we had a private ceremony naming the ball of fur Zelda Sayre Fitzgerald Greenhaw.

She is a Southern cat. As a kitten she followed me. I treated her like a dog. I whistled, she came. I hollered, "Here, Zelda, here!" and she ran for the front door of our little duplex apartment. She walked along beside me when I strolled through Cloverdale and

113

pointed out the house where she was born. I told her about her namesake and how she too could act eccentric, if she wished, because of her name.

I imagine she understood, for she has been an eccentric force in my life ever since. After my young wife skedaddled to a foreign shore, Zelda stayed with her papa. She rode with me when I went on assignments. Once when I traveled to rural Elmore County late at night to interview frightened witnesses who had seen a deputy sheriff beat a black man over the head with a billystick, Zelda came along. She hovered on the top of the seat behind my head and provided company as I waited on a dark and lonely road for the people to arrive.

During afternoons in the late 1960s, when I scouted for locations for a film of a Truman Capote short story, Zelda perched on the seat and watched closely as I perused the countryside. And when another company shot a remarkably bad motion picture, *The Traveling Executioner,* with Stacy Keach, at an abandoned penitentiary near Montgomery, Zelda ran through a scene and destroyed all concentration. The director screamed angrily, and my brief career as a bit player ended abruptly.

I forgave Zelda for her lack of poise before the camera. She took to my sweetheart, Sally Maddox, a lovely assistant attorney general for the state, and even rubbed her furry side against the lady lawyer's stockinged legs. And when Sally and I got married in 1972, Zelda was kept by a friend until we were settled into an apartment in Cambridge, Massachusetts, where I was a Nieman Fellow at Harvard.

Several weeks later Zelda was sent to us. She was drunk from the tranquilizers the vet had given her for the flight. And I think from that moment on Zelda viewed the North through more or less intoxicated eyes.

I took her out in the snow and she played like it was catnip for several minutes, then she sat back and looked up at me with a quizzical expression. She didn't *really* like such foolishness.

In the spring I took her to Soldier Field, a wide expanse of open field in the middle of which stands Harvard's football stadium. I thought she might like to stretch her legs and run next to my feet the way she did back home. But at the first sight of a big dog — everybody seemed to have big dogs at Harvard — she climbed my body like I was the nearest tree. On my shoulder she dug her claws into my skin and hung on for dear life while her body quivered next to my face.

When a friend from Alabama visited, he said he would sleep on the small sofa in our postage stamp-sized living room. Zelda regarded him, shrugged, and moved on about her business. He looked after her and said she'd never had anything to do with him, although he had courted her fancy from time to time.

On the following morning our friend announced gleefully that he had awakened during the night to find Zelda snuggled near his shoulder. "She obviously knew I was home-folks and a friend," he said. I knew she sensed Southern about him and felt comfortable with him because of that.

In May, when we started home, Zelda lay between us on the front seat. On the second full day of driving, as we passed Washington, D.C. and headed into Virginia, Zelda sat up and perked her ears. She looked at me with renewed vitality. She seemed to stretch her legs. She climbed to the back of the seat — her old place for viewing the passing world — and she sat there and showed more and more awareness as we got closer and closer to Alabama.

When we crosed the state line, Sally and I went directly to a restaurant and had big helpings of fried chicken and potato salad. I tore up a piece of white meat and cut it into small bits and took it to the car and gave it to Zelda, who lapped it up quickly.

As we sped down I-85 toward home, Zelda snuggled against my thigh and closed her eyes. After a moment, she was purring softly. She moaned in her sleep and moved closer against me.

At our home in Montgomery she chased birds in our backyard. She crouched low in the high grass like an old hunter. She crept toward her prey but managed only occasionally to catch it.

She spent mornings in the window above my typewriter, just sitting there and providing inspiration. She was happiest in the late afternoon sunlight, lying still and sleeping.

Nowadays she does not venture into the backyard. She no longer stalks through her very own jungle. She doesn't jump from chair to couch. She sleeps a great deal. But she enjoys watching the world outside. She sleeps occasionally on a bookshelf and usually checks out newcomers at any party or get-together we might have. She moves gracefully through the crowd, like a courtly

115

dowager, and now and then rubs her graying coat next to a leg, glancing up more or less seductively.

Note: On the night of May 31, 1987, Zelda, who had been feeling poorly for several weeks, refused to eat. As I held her, she looked up into my eyes and eked deep in her throat. I lay her down and when I went to check on her several hours later she had stopped breathing. I wept profusely, and a good neighbor buried her next to my garage.

Bub Able

Note: My Granddaddy, Bub Able, would have had a great laugh and a lot of satisfaction at having his stories told on the op-ed page of *The New York Times*. As far as I know, he never once read *The Times,* but he always enjoyed good stories. The following was published there on August 6, 1979.

My Granddaddy, Bub Able, was quite a fellow in his day. I remember him well as a storekeeper on the highway south of Birmingham, sitting in the back beyond the great hoop of rat cheese and the Garrett snuff advertisements. He and his friends sat next to the old potbellied stove in the wintertime when it glowed red from the heat of a burning coal fire. They sat back in the cool darkness in the summertime, slowly playing checkers or dominoes, and now and then selling something. Mostly, they talked.

Granddaddy was always weaving a story. I'll never forget the time when a tax man from Montgomery came by and huddled with Granddaddy out beside the high red iron gasoline pump that had a glass tank up on top with a yellow and a green ball inside. I used to love to stand next to the wooden bench under the front shed and watch the yellow and green balls bounce when Granddaddy filled up somebody's tank.

That day was hot as seasoned pepper sauce, the sun laying straight overhead, and Granddaddy, a short, square-built man who leaned slightly to one side and used a walking cane, even took off his felt hat and fanned his face with it. Inside, the band was soaked with sweat, and I knew it had to be an important conversation for him to stand out in the heat that long.

117

When he came inside, he was shaking his head. He was still fanning with the hat.

"What's wrong, Uncle Bub?" one of his younger friends asked.

Granddaddy chomped on his false teeth for a moment, clicking them in his jaw. "I've got to raise the gas," he said.

"What in the world to?" the friend asked.

"Fifteen cents," Granddaddy said. He didn't just say the words, he thought on them, which was his way when things got serious. I had seen him do the same when he talked to Mama or Nanny about some scripture in the Bible that had been troubling him.

"I just don't understand it," Granddaddy finally said. "These roads we've got, they're pretty good. They've just been laid down by Governor (James E. "Big Jim") Folsom. And that man said they've been paid for. He said we've now got to pay for upkeep.

"It sure is something, going up on gas two cents a gallon, just for keeping up a road," he added.

Granddaddy stepped to the door and looked out toward the highway that wound down into the valley and disappeared around a curve.

Back inside, he said that he remembered when gasoline was less than a dime. Settling into his cane-bottom chair and leaning back against a feed sack, he said, "Why, I can well remember my first car. It was a Ford. A-Model. It wasn't much. Cost just under $300."

He looked down at me and wiped the sweat from his brow. "I got it on a Saturday morning. We were living in Tuscaloosa. I drove it to our house, out close to the University, and pulled up and honked the horn. It was loud. Neighbors came out on their porches. Your Mama and Nanny came out. Their eyes were big as saucers. Aw, they had a fit over it.

"I sat up there behind the wheel and said, 'Ya'll want to go for a ride?' Neither one of them could believe that it was really ours. They kept asking me. And they sort of acted like they were afraid of it.

"I cut it off, turned the switch, and I stepped down and offered them a hand. I said that it was indeed ours, and I was also offering them a ride. When it stopped puttering, they allowed as how they would ride — after they had walked around it and looked it over real good.

118

"They got inside and I went around to the front and cranked it up. Off we went with everybody staring at us. I guess I was kind of awe-struck, like a young 'un with a new toy. And I was mighty proud.

"We rode up and down the streets, through town, and you know we were the only ones of one or two dozen in the whole downtown. It wasn't like today when there're ten or twenty cars on every street.

"Finally, I turned us onto a residential street, wanted to show them some pretty homes, and I ran smack into a dead-end street. When we got to the end, I stopped the car and looked around. I pushed one thing and then the other around the steering wheel, but I didn't know how to put the car in reverse. I cut the engine off, walked around, looked it over good, then told the ladies to step down. After they were off, I put my back up against the front end. I lifted. I was strong as an ox back then. I picked that car up, turned it around, and drove off. I never said a word about that to your Mama or Nanny. I just acted like it was the thing to do. The next day I learned how to put that car in reverse." He slapped his knee and laughed at himself.

Note: This story has been reprinted in a half-dozen different anthologies in several different languages.

Teacher And Friend

It happened like it was straight out of the movie life, something perfect.

From a thick fog on the street next to the downtown Tuscaloosa post office stepped a man who appeared taller than he actually was. An expensive old Burberry trenchcoat was draped dramatically over his square shoulders. A narrow-brimmed felt hat sat cocked upon his head. As he went up the steps with an energetic bounce, he looked toward the young boy standing on the stoop.

The man's face was alive with character. His eyes sparkled. His mustache was evenly trimmed. His chin jutted forward as though it had been chiseled from granite.

Moments later the man came out of the post office with the boy's father, who had stopped him and had begun telling him how his son was a writer — just like the man with the draped coat.

The man shook the boy's hand and announced, "I'm Hudson Strode," with stage-like resonance, the words rolling distinctly off his tongue.

The boy stammered his name.

"When were you born?" Strode asked, his voice booming as though he were talking to someone across the street.

The boy said in February.

"Ah, a noble Aquarius!" Strode said.

After a few more moments of conversation, with Strode asking questions and the boy answering, they parted. The boy was embarrassed and didn't speak to his father all the way home.

Several years later, when the boy approached the professor on the campus of the University of Alabama with a manuscript, Strode studied the boy's features.

The boy said that they had met several years back.

"Oh, yes," Strode said, "You're the one with the remarkable father."

Thus began an on-again off-again friendship which, like it happened with so many of his students, warmed and grew closer in the years following schoolday tensions. Strode was an actor. He was a put-on. He had a flare for the dramatic, the overstatement, the need to rid any audience of boredom and give it excitement and enthusiasm. Never once in all the time the boy saw him wearing it did Strode ever put his arms into the sleeves of the trenchcoat.

Strode was very much aware of his signs. "The stars tell us everything," he announced to his chosen few, the 11 or 12 who had been handpicked to sit in his seminar-style classroom three hours every Wednesday night high in the University Library. Born Halloween night of 1892 in Cairo, Illinois, he was raised in Demopolis, attended the University, was a Delta Kappa Epsilon, and went to New York to Columbia and later actually performed Shakespeare drama on the stage.

In his memoirs, *The Eleventh House,* he wrote about his time as a young professor in Tuscaloosa. One of his students, Charlie Johnson of Montgomery, brought him a packet of letters from his girlfriend. "He wanted to read them to me, for he thought they were exceptional," Strode remembered.

"The girl was Zelda Sayre, daughter of a Supreme Court judge. In four years she was to become the wife of F. Scott Fitzgerald. Now she was just sixteen, while Johnson was twenty-one.

"I have always been able to spot talent. The girl had talent to an extraordinary degree. Her letters were original. They had a keenness and a sharpness; they were pungent, slightly racy, and humorous."

A few months later, Strode recalled being met at Montgomery's Union Station by this young woman who was "touched with glamour. I never thought her beautiful, but with her gold hair, green eyes, fine complexion she had something about her that was arresting and even exciting."

His memoirs are as delightful as sitting next to him at his daily afternoon tea in the garden of his home on Cherokee Road in Tuscaloosa. He writes as he talked, full of life and overstatement and names of the famous.

He tells of meeting, getting to know, and becoming dumbfounded with the moody and unpredictable playwright Eugene O'Neill. He speaks of novelists John O'Hara and Ernest Hemingway, off-handedly mentions every touch of royalty in every country in which he traveled, and it is now — in retrospect — delightful. At the time when the students first heard the stories, they seemed pretentious and overblown to the young ears. Today they are happy stories of recollection.

With a fervor of wonderful recognition, he remembers his first class and first success. "In September, 1936, a shy girl named Harriet Hassell, born on a farm on the Watermelon Road in Northport across the Black Warrior River from Tuscaloosa, urged me to permit students in my writing class to do a novel. I said I did not think novel writing could be taught, but she was so eager that I was willing to give it a try."

Her novel, first called *The History of the South* and later *Rachel's Children*, was bought and published by Harper's two years later when it gained generally favorable criticism and a good sale.

Strode wrote 16 books. Perhaps the best known was his multi-volumed biography of Jefferson Davis in which he put to work best his own advice to students: "Reach out! Do not be afraid to display your talent."

With a grandiose twist of his pen, he told about the man he viewed as a tragic hero, a romantic patriot, and a great Southern leader.

In *Timeless Mexico,* he wrote the best history of that country, and in *Now In Mexico* he wove a colorful tapestry of his personal adventures among the who's who south of the border.

However, as a teacher, he excelled. He listened intently as students read their work. Sometimes it was excruciating, listening to the painfully inept sophomoric outpourings of a young man or woman's heartfelt prose, and often he would close his eyes and clasp his fingers before his face, but when the last tear-and-sweat-soaked work was nervously uttered, Strode's face would rise to the occasion like that of a master actor. He spoke out forcefully but never hurtfully. If a story was good but missed the point in the telling, he cut through to the core of the problem and dissected it cleanly.

"See through the character's eyes. Feel through his or her heart. Step in the character's shoes." He made the young writer think. He gave them promise for having been chosen to sit at his table. "You have the talent. Now you must learn what to do with it," he warned.

Those who had the opportunity to study with him in his many writing classes and to experience his making Shakespeare come to life met last spring on the campus of Tuscaloosa. They came together in celebration of Strode to create the Hudson Strode Chair in creative writing.

Successful novelist Borden Deal, who wrote *Dunbar's Cove* from which the film *Wild River* was made and *Bluegrass* about thoroughbred horse racing, remembered, "Hudson Strode was a legend in our time. Every person in the class, I do believe, stood more or less in awe of him. Indeed, he ruled our universe. We devoted more thought, speculation, legend-making, worship, and fear to this god of our creative writing world than to any other person, subject, or theme of our lives.

"Like most gods, Hudson Strude left something to be desired. A small, plump, often self-important man, he was the first real snob I had ever known — the names of kings and princesses and Shakespearean actors fell naturally from his lips.

"He played outrageous favorites. Every year there was in the class a chosen white-haired boy, whom he groomed with tender care for literary stardom. For these favorites, he was known to prescribe diets, attitudes, sleeping and working hours, and to arrange love lives, submissions to and meetings with New York editors, adequate housing, foundation grants, and teaching fellowships.

"I was never Hudson Strode's teacher's pet. Indeed there seemed to exist an unspoken strain of antagonism between us. Yet I respected his criticism, his story sense, and he, I think, respected my talent . . ."

Others, including Thomas Turner of Anniston who wrote the novel *Buttermilk Road* and Carlysle Tillery of Tuscaloosa who wrote *Redbone Woman* in Strode's class, attended the celebration in remembrance of their old professor who died in 1976 in Tuscaloosa.

At the celebration, Montgomery public relations executive Starr Smith reiterated what he had written after Strode's death in

The Independent, "Strode was a tender, understanding, compassionate man. I never found him petty, jealous, or small. True, he was a tremendously hard worker and demanded equal dedication from his writers. His discipline was tight but never harsh. Superb guidance, skilled editorial judgment, and an uplift of the human spirit as well as a careful nurturing of talent was the Strode style. And never in the history of fiction-writing instruction in America has his record been surpassed."

Birmingham's John Forney, author of *Crimson Memories, Golden Days and Other Stories,* told the group gathered at North River Yacht Club, "Hudson Strode would have loved these surroundings. They are serene and they are grand. Here's to a serene and grand individual!" And all hoisted a toast to his memory.

Note: This recollection was printed in the first ALABAMA Magazine I edited and published in March of 1984.

A Man For Many Seasons

When he walks up the incline toward the attractive building that is shaped like an airplane hangar but has a spiffy, modern design, he walks with a swagger.

It is not difficult to see the pilot in the looks of Norman F. McGowin, Jr.

When he sits in the cockpit of his immaculate, superbly restored North American SNJ-6, his rosy cheeks and bright hazel eyes shine with an understanding of this World War II airplane.

Below his cocked elbow is written in bold black: 1/LT. N.F. McGowin, Jr., and he is obviously proud.

Floyd McGowin of Chapman, Alabama, flies the SNJ-6. He takes it up just as he does the bright yellow Stearman Navy trainer biplane that sits nearby.

But it is obviously the SNJ-6 that is his love. It's the one he found after looking for years. He ran into a man at an Elmore County air show who said, "I know where one is in a barn."

Floyd didn't stop until he found the barn on the western side of Camden in Wilcox County. The man who had bought it from the Navy in 1958 for $502 had died. The plane was covered with moss in a hay barn, and the man's brother, who was handling the estate, recognized Floyd as a man who loves airplanes and who would do right by this one.

They struck a deal. It was taken apart piece by piece. It was put back together. And in 1983, it won Reserve Grand Champion at an air show in Oshkosh, Wisconsin.

Now Floyd McGowin is not your everyday flying farmer. He is one of THE McGowins. His father, Floyd Sr., was big in the lumber business, to say the least. His Uncle Earl, who lives in the big columned white house that Floyd's grandfather built, was a Rhodes Scholar and a premier business and political leader.

Before the McGowins sold the family business, W.T. Smith Lumber Company and its hundreds of thousands of acres of timberland, Floyd, who had attended a three-room school in Chapman, prep school up north, and Yale University, managed the woodlands division of the company.

Floyd formed Rocky Creek Logging Company, a name he took from a company that had existed in south Alabama as early as 1884. Today the company handles more than 400,000 cords of wood each year, is involved with timber harvesting, trucking of timber, and has done some creative plantation-thinning in what Floyd sees as "an effective manner."

As a timber farmer, Floyd McGowin has been unique in the usage of airplanes. With several men who work part-time, they have done some 16,000 hours of business flying without an injury to personnel or planes. They fly to detect beetles, using photo mosaics from the air from which they can detect a change in the growth patterns and color changes that might show the beginnings of pine beetles. "We have salvaged thousands of dollars worth of timber each year with this program," he says.

Also, they use the planes — a Beech and a Cessna bush-type — to detect the beginnings of fires in the forests.

During the years, flying has been much more than business for this former Marine who wanted to fly in Korea in the worst sort of way. He dreamed of flying the fighters. He FELT it in his bones. But, according to the Marine bureaucracy, he suffered from high-frequency deafness, a condition which forced him out of service flying.

But it did not preclude his intense love for flying. Here is a man who, when writing about the Douglas AD4-N Skyraider, called it "a big, neat, purposeful design radiating great strength and power; a masculine airplane whose single seat fighter cockpit perched a long way from the ground in a position of commanding visibility."

A board member of First Alabama Bancshares who thinks of airplanes in such terms will work long and hard to surround himself with flying. And surround himself he has.

In his prized hangar, next to the grass landing strip carved from the great pine forest his father and grandfather planted and replanted, he stands beneath huge walls covered with his collection of aviation art. There is a woman who was the first to fly across the English Channel and who was slung to her death because there were no seat belts during that time. There is a black aviator who came within a single strike of making ace.

Floyd McGowin still flies. He flies the Skyraider, DC-3, and P-47 Thunderbolt for the Kalamazoo Aviation History Museum, of which he is extremely proud, for it is in the air that he truly excels.

Inside one section of the hangar are several rooms where he feels comfortable. A modern office looks out onto the strip. The walls are covered with books. There are novels on this shelf about people who fly. In another are stories of French aviators. Then British. German. American. Settling back, Floyd McGowin talks knowledgeably about the books: his favorites, his least favorites.

Across the pond from the airstrip, beyond a strand of virgin pines, his father's home, which he remodeled several years ago, is a comfortable rambling house. It is now his and his wife's, the former Rosa Johnston Tucker of Lexington, Kentucky, a lovely belle who has been at home in Chapman since they were married some thirty years ago.

They have opened the house with picture windows looking out onto the lake, the pines, and the landing strip beyond. Here, again surrounded by books, they enjoy New Orleans-style jazz and their art.

They have raised their children here. Norman F. McGowin III, a graduate of the University of Alabama Medical School in Birmingham, is now a surgeon at Stabler Clinic in nearby Greenville. A daughter, Tucker, is a patient's representative at the UAB Medical Center. And daughter Lucy is married to Dr. Paul Moore, who is presently doing a cardiology fellowship at the UAB Medical School.

With his offices in the old Chapman Hotel, where guests usually arrive via the railroad, Floyd McGowin has created his own world in a universe that had once been owned and controlled by his father, his uncle, and other ancestors. But as one walks and talks with Floyd McGowin, it is suspected that his real world is up there beyond the billowy white clouds. It is a world he knows better than this one under the pine trees. It is his space.

A Country Lawyer

After George C. Wallace was elected governor of Alabama for the second time back in 1970, one of his classmates from the University of Alabama Law School tried to reach him by telephone. Clarence Atkeison, attorney from Prattville, left word with Wallace's secretary.

Two hours later, Wallace Press Secretary Billy Joe Camp returned the call.

Hearing the name, Atkeison boomed, "Billy Joe who? You ain't the one I supported and voted for for governor."

Taken aback, Camp excused himself. Momentarily, Wallace was on the line with a chuckle. He knew that he had done a good job of breaking in his new press secretary. "I can't fool you, can I, Clarence?" he said, and the Governor began listening to Atkeison's request.

After Wallace's two-decade reign, Atkeison said with a smile, "I never got much out of George. But people in Autauga County knew we were friends." He also supported Governor Fob James with "some money and a little talk." A fellow Prattville lawyer said, "Clarence doesn't brag about his political prowess, but if you're running for public office you better stop by his office on Fourth Street and court him a little. Otherwise, you might as well forget the rural Autauga County vote. It's not considerable, but it counts."

Clarence Atkeison was never without the black bowtie, the midnight-dark suit that fit comfortably but loosely, and the red socks that covered his snow-white ankles. He has been practicing his own inimitable brand of country law since the late forties, after he left the University of Alabama in Tuscaloosa, served time in the

Army in England during and after World War Two, and came back to law school and graduated magna cum laude. And he was just as ambitious as he was in the early days.

"I hadn't been practicing law more than several weeks over in my second-story office on Main Street when one afternoon I heard the old wooden steps leading down to the street creaking. I knew it had to be ten or twelve of them. I'd hear one step creak, then another, and another. I didn't know whether they were coming to rob me or offer me a kingship." He laughed heartily and sucked air through his front teeth in a characteristic gesture. "I remembered what an old law professor had once told me, 'If you're ever visited by more than ten folks at one time you've been approached by a mob.'" And he laughed again and sat back.

"By the time they got to the top my office was near about filled with some very distinguished gentlemen," and he names many of the county's prominent citizens. "They said, 'Now, young man, we would like you to run for county solicitor.' I told them I appreciated their thinking so highly of me, but I reckoned I really couldn't qualify since I hadn't lived in the county long enough. They said I shouldn't worry about that, they'd take care of that matter, but I said I really didn't wish to run for public office. But they argued on with me, and I proved stubborn in my position. I told them, 'No, I don't wish to run.'

"One of the older gentlemen said, 'Young man, just what is your ambition?'

"I replied, 'I want to be the best lawyer in Autauga County.' At that time there were only two others and maybe one or two who came in during trial time from Montgomery.

"The old gentleman just looked at me and said, 'Well, you don't have much ambition.'" And he laughed again, the black bowtie bobbing.

In Prattville, a town about seventeen miles northwest of Montgomery, Clarence Atkeison became known among his peers as a fine lawyer. In the town which grew from less than five thousand in the late forties to about twenty thousand in 1984, Atkeison was praised as "the best attorney in these parts before a country jury. He knows how to talk to those people. In a criminal trial or civil suit, he knows how to get down to the nitty-gritty. He talks the jury's language, and it's not put-on," said another local lawyer.

Back in the 1950s he was known as the best in central Alabama, and, although he will not admit it, the word among the lawyers told that he made more than $30,000 annually from criminal work, "and that's better than ninety-nine percent of the criminal lawyers anywhere in the rural South for that period," allows another. "But these days," Clarence said, "one lawyer couldn't make enough to keep him and his family in cornbread and collards on the criminal work in Autauga County. It's all gotten to be court-appointed stuff, and a lot of defendants would rather have a free court-appointed lawyer than somebody who'll charge a little bit and defend them until the sky falls."

Still, he kept his seventy-year-old hands in the courtroom. "Now and then a murder case will come along and they'll walk down here (to his office only one block from the county courthouse) and see me, and I take it on.

"In twenty-five or twenty-six murder cases I've lost two or three. The most any of my clients ever got was eight years, and it was reversed. I guess the most that stuck was seven and a half years. And some of those cases were back when the state was frying folks in the electric chair when they were found guilty of murder.

"I don't like to see anybody but the guiltiest of the guilty go to the penitentiary. I think it's against the grain of human life to cage a man. Some folks need to be taught lessons. That's different. But it really does hurt me to see the innocent being locked behind bars and punished by a hypocritical society," he declared in his deep before-the-jury voice.

"Oh, I have quoted the Bible, I have quoted Shakespeare, and I have quoted some people I didn't even know who I was quoting but it sounded good at the time. Most of these people have never read poetry, much less memorized it, but they near about all have an appreciation for a well-turned phrase. If I can make a point by quoting something, I do it."

In the case of Willie John Henry, a black handyman charged with first-degree murder in the shotgun slaying of a Prattville city policeman, Atkeison pulled out all the stops. "They had his client backed into a corner. The prosecution had proven that Henry was at the scene, had a shotgun in his hand, and the barrel was smoking when the other policeman arrived. In fact, Henry was standing over the body when the other officers got there, and

Henry was immediately arrested," recalled a court clerk. "Clarence had nothing to offer but his client testifying that he shot in self-defense and his own powers of persuasion. In the closing argument, Clarence paced up and down in front of the jury box. He spoke loudly, softly, picked out a woman to talk to, and just like that fell to his knees and coupled his hands under his chin. 'Oh, Lord,' he screamed, and nearly all of the jury left their seats. 'Please guide these poor servants toward a decision of not guilty, Lord. For as you said, Jesus, 'The guilty fleeith while the innocent stand in wait.' Of course, there is no such quote, but the jury let Henry off with a manslaughter conviction and thirty days in the county jail."

Although Atkeison lived in a great rambling brick house he built on a hillside within a stone's throw of downtown Prattville, his favorite place during the years was his beloved Pear Orchard. "I guess every lawyer and other kind of reprobate in central Alabama knows the Pear Orchard," explained fellow Prattville attorney E. Ted Taylor. "That's where Clarence goes to prepare for his cases," Taylor added. And when someone mentioned the Pear Orchard, Atkeison beamed. "It's a wonderful place for contemplation," he said.

Nestled on the banks of the Alabama River, the farmland was covered with pear, peach, and apple trees, several small houses, a year-round muddy catfish pond and two mock graves whose unknown occupants became the subject of countless Atkeison stories. When I asked him about his aunt and uncle, whom he had said once years ago were buried there, Atkeison grinned and shook his head and said, "Did I say that?"

When the homemade whiskey was distilled correctly and given to him by a gracious client or a tenant on another of his farms, Atkeison buried it in hickory-charred kegs in the fresh earth of the Pear Orchard. Some time later, when visited by a reporter or politician or attorney friend, he would personally dig up a keg and pop it. "Now that," he explained with relish, "is pure nectar."

In the mid-eighties, because "I have a heart problem," Clarence gave up the nectar but continued to chain-smoke unfiltered Pall Malls all day long.

His friend Ted Taylor, whose Taylor for U.S. Senate bumper stickers were still on the rear bumper of Atkeison's Lincoln Continental seven years after Taylor's unsuccessful 1978 campaign, said that Atkeison "is one of the most loyal and trustworthy men I have ever known. If he tells you a chicken will pull a plow, you better start hitching him up." And Taylor added that Atkeison was at home at the Pear Orchard or in front of a country jury.

Former Montgomery newsman Tom Cork remembered his first encounter with the lawyer. "I didn't quite know how to take him. He was a courtly gentleman even in his disarray. He invited me very politely to accompany him to the courthouse. He just stuffed sheafs of paper into an old briefcase and crammed several law books on top. After he pushed the books into the case, he looked up and said, 'I won't use these, but it never hurts to have 'em on the table,' and he grinned.

"We walked down to the courtroom and I sat on the front row while he arranged his papers and books on the counsel's table.

"Autauga County deputies brought in some poor old derelict with a grizzly beard and ragged clothing. Clarence turned and ambled over to me and stood next to me and in a stage whisper said, 'Do you know that man?' I said, 'Why, no, Clarence, should I?' and he said, 'Well, I don't know. I don't know him, and I figured he was either a newspaperman or a lawyer.'"

In more recent years, however, his opinions about lawyers mellowed somewhat. "I think most of the young attorneys are doing a fairly good job. But I think too many of them are thinking about making money rather than serving the people. They don't put the people first, and I think a lawyer should always do that. That should be their training," he said.

He never denied making money, but he always lived without the frills of success. During a recess between trials, the late Circuit Judge Joseph Mullins was milling with him and several other lawyers in the hallway of the courthouse. Mullins, making small talk, said, "Clarence, you've made a good deal of money in your day. How have you invested it?" Without hesitating, Atkeison said, "I've got my money tied up in houses and lots, your honor." Mullins, with a solemn face, nodded and said, "Real estate is a wise investment." Without cracking a smile, Atkeison shook his head and said, "You don't understand, your honor — whorehouses and lots of whiskey."

Inside the courtroom, Atkeison labored diligently for the welfare of his client. A fellow lawyer described his work, "Clarence may have fun outside the courtroom. But when he works in front of a jury he is a master. He is the champion of his client. He carries

135

the spear. He is the knight in rather cluttered armor. But he always battles hard for his client. And usually he is very effective."

Asked which case was his favorite, Atkeison pondered the hundreds through the years. When he looked up from his thoughts he said, "Every one you get turned loose is the best. There's not one that's better than all the others."

In years past he defended Ku Klux Klansmen in the mornings and black clients in the afternoons, or vice versa. One of his heroes was the late U.S. Senator J. Thomas "Cotton Tom" Heflin, known for his racist and states rights stands, and his autographed photo decorated Atkeison's law office next to a signed picture of Governor George Wallace. "They were two mighty fine men," Atkeison declared proudly.

While he had not had a KKK client in some time, he quickly pointed out that he believed many Klanspeople were having their Constitutional rights violated by illegal arrests. "I think many of them need better lawyers defending them. They need lawyers who will take the fight all the way to the U.S. Supreme Court if necessary. I believe in all men being given equal protection and due process."

Another classmate from early University of Alabama days was U.S. Circuit Judge Frank M. Johnson Jr., whom Atkeison believed twisted the law to give blacks more than equal rights under the law.

Several years back, when Johnson was presiding judge of the Middle District of Alabama, Atkeison got in a shouting match with a Montgomery lawyer in the federal bankruptcy court. Atkeison and the other man were brought before Johnson, who ordered the U.S. Marshals to put them behind bars together and let them talk over their differences. After about five hours, Johnson called them before him. Glaring over his half-glasses, Johnson asked if they had settled their argument peacefully. "Your honor," Atkeison said, "we have been sitting and we have been talking. If you send us back, we'd sit and we'd talk, if we could find anything to talk about. But, your honor, I would like for you to take judicial knowledge of the fact that I did not call him a liar. What I said was, 'What he said was false *ab initio.*'" The judge found both men in contempt and fined them one hundred dollars each. When the other attorney asked if he could write a check, the judge said the court did not accept personal checks. Atkeison pulled two one hundred dollar bills from his pocket and paid his opponent's fine without another word.

In the late 1970s, a woman who had been his legal secretary told about another of his eccentricities. One afternoon while cleaning the office she flipped through an old law book and found fifteen one hundred dollar bills. Asked about the incident, Atkeison shrugged and allowed, "I used to hide money around here all the time, but I don't do that anymore."

He said that "if I had all the money people owe me I could retire tomorrow" and pointed to several bad checks — one for five hundred dollars and another for twenty-five dollars — pinned to the wall behind his chair. And from behind a picture he pulled another twenty-five dollar bad check dated 1968.

"You don't work for money only," he said. "Being a lawyer has been a good profession for me." In the background, a woman stepped into the reception room with four wooden straight-backed chairs and a sign reading: Be seated, Be quiet or Be gone. She gave the secretary a check for rent on a house Atkeison owned. It was one of many.

Leaning back and clasping his hands behind his head, Atkeison began another story about another trial in which he took the state's number one witness and led her around a verbal block. "By the time she was through she was so confused she didn't know whether she was wearing a dress or was stark naked on the evening the murder took place. The jury was laughing at the poor woman. And my client went free because the jury didn't believe her incriminating testimony," he added, and he grinned and winked.

Hawk Eyes

I had heard about Judge Matthew Debrough all of my life. Granddaddy used to talk about him when he and the other men gathered around the red-hot pot-bellied stove in the back of the store. Granddaddy had a cane-backed rocking chair where he'd sit and rock and talk, when he wasn't playing dominoes or checkers or tending to the wants of a customer. Over behind him on the wooden counter was always a partial hoop of cheese and an open box of soda crackers. You could get a bite of cheese and your fill of crackers for a nickel and drink a soda pop with it for a dime. Once in a while somebody'd come in with a bulging pocket and silently pass around a fruit jar of the vilest smelling liquor and now and then the Smalley boys brought in a six-pack of Schlitz and shared them. Granddaddy'd take a drink, but he didn't care for beer; said it gave him gas and he didn't like gas.

They got to talking about Judge Matthew Debrough on this Tuesday afternoon in early May not more than an hour after J.R. North rode up in his three-year-old Studebaker and lifted the trunk and showed us the hawk he'd shot up on Godfrey's Ridge. I was still sort of shaken by the sight, so I didn't catch the first few words about the Judge. When J.R. came, he was jubilant and jumped out of the car like he had ants in his pants and threw open the trunk and said, "Look here, Uncle Bub!" Everybody around Samantha Station called Granddaddy Uncle Bub, whether they were kin to him or not. I rushed out and looked down at the mass of feathers and the once-powerful beak and flat forehead that now lay dormant in the dust of J.R.'s trunk. The eyes poked out of the feathery skull. Black eyes stared directly at me with a deathly coldness that chilled my shoulders. As I looked at the brown-

139

speckled wide pale breast, J.R. reached down and pulled out a wing to show a span of nearly six feet. I just gasped. Eyes wide, I reached out to touch the wing where it joined the body, and when I did, the wing flapped. I swear it did! That bird was supposed to be dead. You could see where J.R. had shot it in the back, where blood streamed across the red dirt caked on the floor of the trunk, but still that wing flapped, and I jumped back and caught my breath high in my throat. I held my right hand in the cradle of my left palm. Lord knows what a big bird like that could do if he caught you just right!

Now, with the copper taste of fright still in my mouth, they were talking about Judge Debrough passing the sentence of death on a black man named Tom Fowler. "What in the world did he do?" I uttered, amazed that a Negro judge would put such a sentence on another of his kind. "Killed a man," Mister J. Edgar Hughes said. "Over a saddle," James Larkin said. Granddaddy, clutching his wooden cane in his hands between his legs, said, "Old Tom Fowler saw this man Jeffers McDonald riding out of Northport on this brown mule and walked up to him and said, 'I like that saddle you got on that mule.' And when Jeffers McDonald didn't climb down and offer to turn it over to him right on the spot, Tom Fowler leveled his double-barrel on him and blew him out of that hand tooled saddle." Mister J. Edgar shook his head slowly and said, "That's a mean sonofabitch for you." Granddaddy said, "Yes, is. And what's more, Tom Fowler just reached up and ungirthed that saddle and slid it off the mule's back. He slapped the mule on its haunches and sent him on his way. He took his old saddle off his roan horse and fixed the new saddle on and rode off, leaving the old saddle laying right there. I reckon at least four or five people saw what'd taken place, and all of 'em told Judge about it and he passed sentence. They say it didn't take more 'n a minute to make his mind up."

I was sitting on a Coca-Cola case and leaned forward and said, "But he ain't no real judge, Granddaddy." Granddaddy nodded. "To them he is," said Mister J. Edgar. "He's the oldest and the strongest," Granddaddy said.

I never disputed Granddaddy, but I thought on it. I had seen Judge Matthew Debrough sitting on the front proch of his big unpainted house over on the far side of Godfrey's Ridge. He was a sight: a big, heavy man with real long but skinny arms, an Adam's apple the size of my fist, with sunken cheeks that were light tan, like an Indian's skin. He had eyes big around as half-dollars, and they poked out from dark circles like they were on stems. He was old. His skin looked like it was glued to the bones. He never looked strong to me.

"When the Judge passes sentence, that's it," Granddaddy said, and so the talk turned to who was going to be the next county commissioner, and every one of them had a different opinion.

At supper I tried several times to ask Nanny something about Judge Debrough, but she just said, "Hush and eat your chicken and dumplings." Granddaddy talked about the dry spell and how we needed rain in the worst sort of way, and after we finished he settled in his chair in the living room, unbuckled his britches, consulted the Farmer's Almanac, and turned on Fibber McGee and Molly. I knew better than to interrupt his favorite radio program, so I just lay on the rug and listened to the carryings on in the McGee household.

I woke up once during the night and lay very still and listened to the trucks on the highway and watched the reflection of their lights travel across the ceiling. I had dreamed about Judge Debrough. He was sitting on his porch and looking down at me with powerfully weird eyes. When he started to speak he croaked like a wounded bird, and when I ran away, he stood. I looked back and he sprouted great gray wings and flew toward me and swooped low with the talons of a six-foot-tall falcon reaching down to claw me.

I got out to the store earlier than usual and had a hold of the broom and was sweeping out the back. I said to Granddaddy, who was counting change, "I been wondering about Judge Debrough."

"He's a right powerful figure in the North River valley," Granddaddy said.

"What makes him powerful?" I said, leaning against the broom and staring up toward the cash register where he was counting out change.

"He makes himself powerful by his actions," Granddaddy said. "He's a deliberate man."

I thought on that for a spell, pushing the broom into the dust.

"Back when Ada Lee and her boy Tom Tom got bad sick, Judge Debrough sent somebody down to see about them," Granddaddy

141

said. "He prayed for them and let them know he did, and then he made up a potion."

"A potion?"

"He fancies himself a medicine man."

"I thought he was a judge."

"He's got lots of power," Granddaddy said softly.

James Larkin came in and started on about how it looked like storms were brewing up in the north "and we're likely to get blowed away by nightfall." Granddaddy said he didn't reckon that'd happen, since we had a pretty good hold on things and he had provisions in the storm pit. "They's going to be some bad tornadoes," James Larkin predicted. "I hear tell Tupelo, Mississippi, got struck by a whipper last night and not much left but some low-lying houses."

After he left, I asked Granddaddy if he wanted me to check on the storm pit, but he said everything was okay, for me not to worry, and he turned the radio to the station with the most up-to-date news coverage.

I went out the back door and stood in the yard and looked out at about the bluest sky I'd ever seen. You wouldn't think a storm would hit in a hundred years, but I knew you just couldn't tell on an early spring day; anything liable to happen.

In the afternoon the men didn't show for their usual game, so I went across the dirt road to the barnyard and scratched the old lazy sow behind the ear, and she put her head down and sort of moaned. I sat on the top board of the wooden fence and looked down at her and told her I was going to find out all about Judge Matthew Debrough and she just looked at me and put her head down again.

It wasn't long before the sow that was swollen with piglets in her belly began moving around the pen nervously, kicking her short legs against the clay and snorting dust. I looked out to the northwest and saw it coming, black as soot against a gray sky, whipping up madly far above the treetops.

I scampered down and ran for the store and burst through the back door. "It's coming," I hollered.

"Settle down," Granddaddy said. "Go get Nanny and meet me at the storm pit. I'll lock things up here."

I took off running across the yard, under the twin water oaks, up the steps, and shouted at the screen door, "Nanny, come on!

We've got to go to the storm pit!" and she came out with her apron bundled in her lap, wiping flour from her hands.

As we moved through the yard we heard the rustling sound in the oaks. Leaves brushed together and whistled loudly. It grew louder and louder, and by the time we pushed the door of the pit back against the red clay and the board that formed a frame, the storm roared like a dozen horses trampling the ground above our heads.

I held to Nanny as she settled back in the far corner on the stool next to the shelves of can goods and bottled water that we changed every few weeks during tornado seasons. She patted my back and said, "Everything's all right," in her low, reassuring tone, but the roar of the storm roared even louder, like the freight train crossing the highway going into Birmingham. It gave me the willies, like the freight train had when I stumbled upon the tracks out in the big woods over the hill this side of the blackberry patch. I had been standing there, knowing I had never wandered that far from home, and I was only six years old at the time and knew I couldn't tell Granddaddy I'd gone that far, and all of a sudden I heard the clickety-clacking sound against the shiny iron rails and I backed up against the trunk of a sycamore, and I shivered until the great huge train rumbled on past. For more than a year I never went that far again, but I dreamed about the sound of it and the way it shook the ground, and now I knew there was something even worse outside.

When the train came around the swell of the hillside and headed toward me, I knew I would be crushed against the big tree. Now the ground shook the same way. My grip on Nanny tightened. She hugged my shoulders and let me cling to her. Granddaddy shuffled around, getting himself situated in his chair.

The door shook like a giant had ahold of the latch and was wrestling with it. It rattled and tore loose at the bottom, and then it made more racket, and I thought I was going to climb up into Nanny's lap like I did when I was little.

The noise took a dip. It sounded more like a swooshing than a smashing. Then the roar growled, and just as I looked around, the door sucked away like it was a splinter being jerked out of a pine board. I thought I was going to cry out, but I also knew I wouldn't. I held the lump midway in my throat and didn't let it go. It was something that Granddaddy had taught me during the years, that when you're truly afraid you hold the sound of the fright inside and that way you're more brave and true to yourself. That way the fright would go away and you would still be whole, and you would be comforted by the very thought.

I held tightly to Nanny and said nothing.

The sound died. It quieted to a deathly emptiness, and I was suddenly not sure which was worse: the roar or the silence.

Granddaddy was the first to move. He pushed through a pile of debris, kicking away dirt and leaves and lifting aside broken limbs and tree branches.

I followed close behind Nanny.

Granddaddy's silhouette was great against a hazy late afternoon sun, and I gazed around the mound of Nanny's big hips toward the sad sight of our house without a roof. The storm had reached down and picked it up and laid it just as pretty as you please over in the pasture on the other side of the barnyard and pig pen. It sat there and didn't look from here like one nail was missing.

Nanny uttered, "I declare."

Granddaddy said, "Let's see what else," and he hobbled toward the house.

None of us said a word. The wind was quiet. The world was silent as a funeral.

The front yard was swept clean. Against the side of the store, under the Garrett Snuff sign, a pile of tin cans, cords from Nanny's clothesline, Prince Albert cans, and tattered clothes from the back porch looked as though they had been stacked there.

The sow lay in her pen and stared at us through tiny eyes, and I went to the barnyard and saw that she did not move. Nearing her, cold bumps covered my spine and froze me deadstill. "Gran . . ." I managed.

He was at my side momentarily and moved ahead and bent to the mound of hairy wet flesh.

What happened, none of us knew; over supper, after I picked up junk that had been scattered, after Granddaddy had straightened the store, and after Nanny had rushed through the house to find not one thing out of order, Granddaddy surmised that the sow had had a heart attack; but he didn't know for sure.

Following supper, we went to the radio. I recognized an uneasiness in Granddaddy, and I didn't bother to turn on Sky King or the Lone Ranger.

I was in my pajamas ready for bed when a sound of metal scraping against metal clanked outside, and there was a jingle of harnesses and the lowing sound of a sad cow.

At the front window in the living room I stared out into the twilight darkness.

Nanny stepped onto the front porch, drying her hands on her apron, and Granddaddy hobbled behind her, and I stood behind him and looked around his thick middle.

Two big horses pulled a wagon behind which a brown milk cow was tied. The cow was stretching her neck and opening her mouth, and she looked as though her entire body was in pain. Her eyes were dark and damp.

Atop mattresses piled and tied high over several old chests of drawers on the wagon sat a big fat black man with a bald head that reflected the bright shine of the setting sun. He had huge round eyes and a full African nose. He looked toward us and raised his right hand like the peace sign from a picture show Indian.

When Granddaddy went onto the porch, I stood in the shadows. Judge Matthew Debrough said, "It took the house." The little cricket-faced woman who drove the team of horses said they'd stay with her sister until everything was fixed back the way it'd been before the storm.

The Judge's expression never changed. He looked out across the tops of the horses' heads, through the cocked ears. He looked with those huge popped-out eyes that I dreamed about that night. "The men'll be here in the morning and 'll help with that roof," he said. "Much obliged," Granddaddy said, and the woman slapped the reins against the horses' backs and they jangled down the road.

The next morning, J.R. North stopped at the store, had Granddaddy fill 'er up, and swigged at his Coca Cola. "Was a rough 'un yesterday," he said, cutting himself a wedge of cheese from the hoop.

"Ran Judge Debrough and his woman out of their place," Granddaddy said.

"Flattened it, like a fritter," J.R. said.

Granddaddy told how they'd come by and where they said they'd be.

"The weirdest thing," said J.R., "was what happened to Tom Fowler."

Granddaddy frowned. "What happened?" he said.

145

I worked my way closer behind the counter.

"They found him after the storm."

"Up at his house?"

"Right in the front hallway. Not a piece of furniture out of place. Just like nothing had happened whatsoever. When all the racket started, his old woman and the children hit the pit out back. Tom didn't make it out of the house, they said. When it was all over, he was laying there on the floor. A piece of pine sapling about this big around . . ." He circled his thumb and forefinger, ". . . had gotten tore off the way it sometimes does. That piece of fresh wood with the sap still flowing through it was stuck right into Tom Fowler's heart."

Granddaddy shook his head real slow.

I backed deep into the shadows of the wooden bin where he kept dried beans.

J.R. North finished drinking his pop and put the bottle with a clink onto the counter. He paid and walked outside, and a silence came over the store like the one right after the storm.

Alabama Ghosts

I saw a ghost.

My roommate, Joe Martin, one of the premier radio announcers in Montgomery, and I moved into an ancient mansion on the corner of Goldthwaite and Mildred streets in the spring of 1967. We had to wait to move into our apartment while the owner of the house, J. Winter Thorington, moved out. We watched while much of his furniture, including a baby grand piano, was stored in a front room where there was also a great four poster bed made of solid mahogany and a big impressive oil portrait of his beautiful gray Persian cat Smokie, who was buried in the garden behind another apartment.

On Monday afternoon, after we had finished completing our moving in on Sunday, Joe and I fixed our first drink of the evening. We went onto the stone patio where we started a fire in our portable barbecue. We clicked gin-and-tonics, drinking a toast to the great times we could see unfolding before our bachelor eyes for this magnificent, roomy, alluring apartment.

Just as we touched the glasses to our lips, I saw something above Joe's head. It was actually atop the fence which surrounded our garden-patio. It was a gray head of a woman with long white hair. She was peering down at me with an almost blank but somehow curious expression.

Joe said, "What is it, man?" Later he said my face had changed suddenly to the damndest look he'd ever seen on anybody's face. He knew I saw something that scared me half out of my wits.

I pointed toward the face that was looking from the top of the high fence which was made with two layers of concrete blocks on

147

top of which large doors from old Montgomery houses had been placed. It was at least ten feet high.

When Joe wheeled around, the face disappeared.

"You go that way, I'll check down here," I said. He went to the gate which was latched nearest the house. It connected our garden with the one for a rear apartment. I ran to the western end of the long garden and opened another latched gate there. We met on the other side. Neither of us had seen a thing nor had we heard any movement. The only other gate out of that garden was an iron gate which made a loud noise when it was opened and closed.

It was in this garden that we had earlier been shown the small but elaborate gravestone for Smokie, the beloved cat of Winter and his friend.

"Maybe it was a cat," Joe suggested when we got back into our own garden.

I shook my head. "No," I said. I described it again: it was like a translucent woman, but it wasn't threatening; it was just there.

As one can imagine, the sighting was cause for conversation for some time afterward. And, of course, I wouldn't let it rest. After all, I was a reporter and was naturally curious. I asked everyone who lived in the house if they had seen any kind of ghost.

Johnny Johnson, who lived in the apartment behind us in the oldest part of the house which was first built in 1853, said he had never seen anything but had heard movement on the second floor. As it turned out, however, the second floor was boarded off and it had no flooring over the support beams. In other words, no one could walk there and make the type of sounds Johnny heard. The flooring had been taken out in the twenties or thirties, according to our landlord, who had moved to the Carolinas.

Another tenant, Jimmy Evans, a young lawyer who was later to become city judge and district attorney, said he had heard several spooky sounds but had never actually seen a ghost.

About two weeks after I had seen the woman's face looking at me I was lying in bed reading when I heard the sound of a piano playing. I sat up in bed. I listened intently. I was sure the sound was coming from the room next to mine. But I had seen Winter Thorington padlock that room where the piano had been stored.

The sound I heard was that of an accomplished pianist. This was no amateur, and the piano seemed perfectly in tune for some rather elaborate runs up and down the keyboard. I did not recognize the number, but it was something classical and complex.

I slipped on my trousers, went outside and around to the front of the house. I rang the doorbell downstairs to the upstairs apartment, and the two young women who lived there buzzed me in.

As I walked by the door to the storage room in the entrance hallway, the music had disappeared. The door to the room was still locked. I went up the stairs and told the women what I'd heard. They said they had heard nothing.

Much of that night I slept fitfully, awakening now and then to face the wide sliding doors that separated my bedroom from the room where the piano was stored. Those doors had earlier been locked securely from inside the storage room.

I heard not another sound. All was quiet. The night was simply dark and filled with the subtle sounds that can oftentimes grow loud in an old house.

The portion of the house where we lived, which had been renovated and made into apartments in the late 1950s, was added to the original house in 1870. And the second floor above us, where the two young women lived, was added several years after that.

The original house, a rectangular two-storied affair that looked like a cross between Italianate and French country chateau, had a sixteen-foot-deep moat and a basement where it was said slaves were once kept. Behind this house was a twenty-two-by-twenty-two square building with a fireplace in the middle. This had originally been the kitchen. In modern times it had been restored as a fashionable architect's office, but by the time we moved to Winter Place it had been allowed to digress into disrepair.

The architect, who had lived with his wife and young daughter in the back apartment where Johnny Johnson now lived, told the story about how one evening he was babysitting with his young daughter while his wife attended a meeting. As he was playing with the little girl, her eyes scanned the floor slowly. When her eyes fixed on the doorway to the garden, she turned back to her father and said, "Who was that lady, Daddy? It wasn't Mama."

The architect and his wife decided they would not question the child about the incident, not wanting to frighten her or leave her with a frightened impression.

Another couple, Judith and Mercer Helms, both of whom worked at *The Montgomery Advertiser* at the time, said they had witnessed the work of what they presumed to be poltergeists when they lived in the small one bedroom apartment in the front section. "We would leave and the brass candelabrum that we had on the fireplace would be moved to the floor. They would still be standing upright but they would always be moved," said Mercer, who later became a professional magician and moved to California. Once, Judith said, the clock from their bedside table flew across the room, but she insisted that it was not thrown in a belligerant manner, it merely floated.

Two young men who moved into the same small apartment said they had seen lighted candles floating across the living room and had experienced their stove going off in the middle of cooking a meal. "It's aggravating little things that just tend to make you mad, but later you laugh at them," said one.

Who was the ghost? I wondered.

Legend had it that the house was haunted by a young man who had committed suicide at Winter Place after he was spurned by Winter Thorington's cousin, Elizabeth Winter Watts. Others said that Sallie Gindrat Winter Thorington, J. Winter Thorington's mother, who lived for more than sixty years, until her death on December 31, 1935, in the house, had been seen rocking in a second floor window. "I knew it was her," one Montgomery matriarch told me. "I knew her well and knew the way she sat, and I would swear that was her, long after 1935."

Among those who frequented parties at the house were the young belles of the early 1900's: Zelda Sayre, Tallulah Bankhead, Sarah Haardt, Sara Mayfield, and others. Of course, Zelda later married F. Scott Fitzgerald, whom she escorted to at least one party at Winter Place, which it was said became the setting of more than one Fitzgerald short story. When H.L. Mencken came south to marry Sarah Haardt, one reception was held at Winter Place. And Sara Mayfield, who wrote biographies of the Fitzgeralds and the Menckens, recalled that Winter Place was her favorite residence in Montgomery. "I believe a female ghost of any one of a dozen women I knew during that time could haunt Winter Place," she said in later years.

While the lady over the fence remained the only ghost I have ever seen, the fascination with ghosts was with me since I was a

150

small boy. My Granddaddy used to tell me about the ghost of a child who haunted the old Samantha Elementary School.

The child's father, who was a drunkard, carried the little boy to the dark and empty schoolhouse on a moonless November night to punish him for coming home late. Actually the boy had stopped on his way home from school to help a neighboring farmer with his cattle in order to make extra money, since the ten-year-old was never given a solitary cent by his father.

To punish the boy, the angry father locked him in a broom closet and left him at the school.

The next morning, when the school was opened by the principal and teacher, they heard a deep-throated moan. They opened the classroom door and heard it more distinctly. They broke the padlock on the door to the broom closet, opened the door, and discovered it empty. But the moaning stopped.

When the other children came to school the boy from down the road was not with them. When the boy's father came to fetch him, the man was told that his son never came to school.

The father went to the closet and opened it. In the darkness inside, a moaning sound cried out. The man slammed the closet door.

The boy was never again seen in the community, although on moonless nights he howled like a wolf from the inside of the dark schoolhouse.

Sometimes, the children said, they heard his footfalls inside the empty schoolhouse when they got there before the teacher or the principal. They said he walked back and forth, back and forth.

After Granddaddy told me the story, I imagined what a horrible man the father must have been. But I never saw him. He died long, long ago, they said, when his North River house caught fire late one moonless night in November.

Late at night, when we went camping out in the big woods, far back over the hills and hollows on the banks of a willow-shaded creek, Granddaddy would tell the story. My brother Don and I would huddle close, look into each other's darkly lighted eyes, and shiver with the eerie sound of the story still in our ears. By the next morning, it was always funny how the sleeping bags of all the boys who were camping out were pushed close together until they were touching. That was one way you could always tell if it was a really good ghost story.

Also when I was a boy I would visit my paternal grandparents in Town Creek in the summertime. My Aunt Lucy was good friends with Miss Annie Wheeler, the elderly daughter of General Fighting Joe Wheeler. She had snow white hair and delicate hands. When she told the story of the ghost in the castle her hands accentuated the words.

Once upon a time, she said, there was a beautiful young girl who lived in the castle between Town Creek and Moulton. It was a yellow brick mansion with a high round yellow brick tower from which the girl's father looked out over the thousands and thousands of acres of his plantation. From this vantage point the man, who was a tyrant with the many slaves he owned, kept a close watch on all the crews he sent out over the vast bottomland of the Tennessee River. He knew exactly who worked and who loafed.

Miss Annie told the story with great details, including a description of the young girl with long blonde hair that danced around her dainty shoulders in ringlets, sparkling green eyes that reflected as beautifully as crystal-clear pools, and skin the shade of perfect ivory. She described how the girl went riding across the fields on her sleek black mare, sitting sidesaddle like the absolute gentle lady, which she was, and how she courted suitors on the portico overlooking the formal English gardens tended by the yard slaves.

Miss Annie told about the father becoming angry with one slave whom he caught loafing instead of working. The man, a particular favorite of the pretty young daughter, was actually sitting down because his foot had been bitten by a snake and he was doctoring himself. But the angry plantation owner would listen to no reasoning and banished the slave to work in the far, far corner of the cottonfields.

As the black man limped off, the girl begged her father to forgive him. But the man said, "No! He must be punished!"

With hoe in hand, the slave limped across the wide field.

That night the young girl slipped out of the castle and saddled her horse and rode away across the field.

The next morning, when the owner climbed up into his tower, he could not find the slave, even when he used his spyglass which he had bought from a riverboat captain.

152

At the breakfast table he was told that his daughter was missing. She had ridden off on her horse and had disappeared in the middle of the night.

He searched high and low, but he never could find the girl or the slave. For years he looked and looked. He sent out parties to search for them through Alabama to the south, Tennessee to the north, and even into the westward frontier lands. He posted rewards, but no one ever claimed them.

It was said that the girl gave her horse to the slave and she attempted to swim the river but was sucked into the deep by the harsh current. It was said, Miss Annie told us, that on a windy night a body could hear the hoofbeats of the horse across the northernmost acres of the man's property. And at just the right spot on the riverbank, a careful listener could still hear the girl calling for help.

As we rode by the crumbling castle and the silhouette of the partial tower, my eyes fixed on them and the woods surrounding them. At night I sat on Aunt Lucy's porch and looked out across the flat fields toward the place where the castle sat, and I listened intently to the wind.

Once, at a Montgomery family reunion at a picnic area which is now Wheeler State Park, I sat on the banks of the great river and threw pebbles into the dark water and listened. Just as I was about to walk back to the picnic area, I thought I heard the cry of a young girl from across the wide water, but I was never sure.

There were many other ghost stories that have been recalled by people throughout Alabama. There was the sound of the mysterious boat in Mobile Bay, a chugging and a hooting of the horn and a calling of "Ahoy!" on certain foggy midnights when a full moon cast gray-black shadows upon the surly water. There was the Encanchata Indian warrior who stood watch on the high bluff overlooking the Alabama River when tugboats pushed heavy barges around big bends west of Montgomery. There was the hillbilly singer's plaintive voice yodeling in the northeastern hills of DeKalb County where his sweetheart had run away with a mountain man.

All of these are as resonant as the state itself, begging to be heard over and over again, echoing into gentle nights, until in the very telling they became true and real and meaningful to the listener and the teller.